Praise for *Good Sport*

'Finally, a book that specifically focuses on how to speak with your kids, before, during and after an athletic event. There isn't a more relevant book for sports parents and coaches on the market today. The lessons in it will help your young athletes perform better on the field, and become healthier human beings off it.'
—John O'Sullivan, Founder,
Changing the Game Project

'Dr Jay-Lee's book *Good Sport* is a treasure chest of practical and proven ways to help your child athlete to stay focused on the process when there are so many distractions around them. Much more than a self-help book, this book is destined to be the definitive guidebook for parents, and a tried and true handbook for teachers and coaches.'
—Lawrie Montague, PGA Professional

'Sport governing bodies and coach accreditation program directors worldwide should consider it as compulsory reading. Easily the best in its genre, this book represents a welcome and timely antidote to results-outcome driven processes, particularly when competitive age ranges are getting younger.'
—Dr Sandy Gordon, Sport Psychologist,
Performance Perspectives International

'Jay-Lee has written a book that is a must read for any parent or supporter of a young athlete, giving valuable advice and strategies to help guide conversations and improve outcomes. I see *Good Sport* as an essential resource in the sporting landscape and highly recommend its use by anyone that has a vested interest in supporting their athlete regardless of the level reached.'
—Jade Edmistone, Founder ONCORE Academy,
Former Australian Swimmer 3 × World Champion
and 5 × World Record Holder

'This book offered me so many *ah-ha* moments of experiences I have had coaching athletes through a variety of sports. It is one of the most important coaching books I have read. With practical tools to implement, it has become my go-to resource for the mental skills side of coaching.'
—Kirsten Norden, Swimnastics, Founder and Coach

'Dr Jay-Lee offers deep insight into the mind of this generation's young athletes and how parents and coaches can work with them on the journey and help to develop true passion for sport and the self-confidence to compete.'
—Barry Prime, International Olympic Swimming
Coach now specialising in swimming development

'There isn't a resource on the market today for coaches and parents quite like this one. The insights and strategies Dr Jay-Lee offers are powerful. A must read.'
—Chris Nesbit, Olympic Coach and
Head Coach of Carlile Swimming

'The practical tips, techniques and advice Jay-Lee shares are pertinent not just on the sidelines of sport, but also as a supporter of your child's development through their journey of life! Before reading this book, I used to dismiss my eldest daughter's pleas for me to just sit quietly, not yell comments and basically stop being embarrassing. From now on, you'll find me practising my "attentive silence" from the sidelines and offering a gentle nod or pre-determined, non-embarrassing, subtle fist pump instead!'
—Karina Newmarch, Olympian and Parent of
two budding athletes

'For a lot of junior athletes and their parents there is a time when it goes from being "just for fun" to "being serious" and sometimes that will happen very quickly. *Good Sport* examines and analyses some of the pitfalls and uncertainties lurking during these times and explains how to navigate and build a plan in what is an extremely important part of the journey that might be for many 10+ years in the making.'
—Gregory R Anketell, PGA Professional,
High Performance Coach

'To access Jay-Lee's expertise in book-form is an absolute blessing. Her wealth of experience mentoring psych skills specific to adolescent athletes is now bound between pages! Having been an Australian representative athlete, and now with children of my own, I'm so grateful that this tool is available.'
—Rachel Smith, Australian Paddle Sports Champion

'To be able to share this information in this book with my four boys will be a privilege and it's narrated in an simple-to-understand way. To all the future stars, everyone needs a Dr Jay-Lee in their corner.'
—Simon Leslie, CEO and Author of *White Belt
Mentality, Equanimity: There is No F in Sales*

'Dr Nair shares her first-hand experiences both as an athlete and as a sports psychologist to present clear, concise and effective strategies that are applicable in all forms and at all levels of sporting and athlete development.'
—Danny Tauroa, Director of Sport,
Student-Athlete Coach, Educator

'Essential reading for all parents and coaches who wish to maximise their know-ledge of the complexities involved in the development of youngsters in sport.'
—Ian Turner, Former Head Coach Great Britain
and Singapore Swimming

Dr Jay-Lee Nair is an Australian sport psychologist who has lived and worked in Singapore since 2012. Her area of expertise is working with young athletes who experience performance anxiety; teaching them strategies to thrive in the competitive environment.

Dr Jay-Lee's Masters and doctorate degrees focused on the study of perfectionism in sport. When she moved to Singapore she found herself in the 'perfect' place to support high achievers and perfectionists in a very competitive results-focused nation. Her practice there has fuelled her passion in the area of psychology and compelled her to share these insights in my book.

Originally from Perth, Dr Jay-Lee completed her first two degrees in psychology in the United States, while accepting an athletic scholarship to play NCAA Div-1 collegiate golf. She finished with academic all-American honours, and attributes her career as a sport psychologist to the success she achieved in both sport and studies.

Good Sport is Dr Jay-Lee's first book.

jay-lee.com

DR JAY-LEE NAIR

GOOD SPORT

How to support and talk to young athletes
before, during and after the game

brio
BOOKS

ISBN 9781761282256

This international edition is published by:

Brio Books, an imprint of Booktopia Group Ltd
Unit E1, 3-29 Birnie Avenue, Lidcombe, NSW 2141, Australia
briobooks.com.au

In association with Bernadette Foley, Broadcast Books, www.broadcastbooks.com.au

Printed and bound by Lightning Source

booktopia.com.au

TABLE OF CONTENTS

CHAPTER ONE
THE NUTS AND BOLTS

Parents, teachers and coaches, I wrote this book for you. I hope it will support you in your journey alongside your children, and the children you teach and coach, as they play sport at any level. While you will pick up mental skills throughout *Good Sport* that you can introduce to your young athletes, it is not intended to be a guide for teaching children the strategies or techniques used in sport psychology. Instead, I provide practical tools and techniques you can use to conduct positive debriefing sessions, collaborative reflections and even casual conversations with young athletes. The aim is *not to teach*, but to shepherd your child's focus, goals and expectations in a way that helps them to thrive in competition, and enjoy and even love the sport they play.

This is your game changer for shaping truly supportive messages and conversations before, during and after the game.

The tough truth is that your children – your young athletes – can be highly resistant to advice and direction from their parents, coaches and teachers. Taking this into account, in the following chapters I suggest realistic ways you can shape collaborative conversations about their sport endeavours that can strengthen your relationship with these players.

I recognise the distinct role of the coach as the instructor and teacher, and the parent as the supporter and facilitator, but *not* in a passive way. Parents, you should feel empowered, especially when you consider the sacrifice and commitment you make in your role. This book introduces ways to *actively* build your child's self-awareness and help them capitalise on defining moments and experiences in their sports journey.

Good Sport is for:

- invested sport parents who want to be a part of their athlete's sport journey, no matter how far they go
- parents who have been told 'It's better you don't come to my matches anymore'
- parents who are just as frustrated as their athletes with the debrief during the car ride home after the game
- parents who are perplexed about what to say and what not to say, so have resorted to saying nothing at all
- coaches who want to develop a self-driven athlete who can independently manage the competition arena
- teachers wishing to avoid dictating to their students what their sport aspirations should be
- anyone who supports a child who experiences performance anxiety.

My own path

Born and raised in Perth, Australia, I am an athlete myself. I played Division One collegiate golf in the US with a full athletic scholarship. When I completed my doctoral degree in sport psychology, I was determined to establish my career as a psychologist in sport on a full-time basis. That was instead of the traditional path of teaching and research with a sprinkling of consulting here and there, or private practice on the side. I loved the process of research and was committed to my research on perfectionist personality types in sport and exercise, but I felt isolated. I wanted more interaction with others, and I believed I had a lot to offer in the counselling space.

So, in 2012 I moved to Singapore to take on a full-time role as the resident psychologist at the newly founded, world-class facility of the Singapore Sports School. It is dedicated to developing local talent and is a shining example of the government's focus on developing sport in the country. Education is extremely important in Singapore culture and there is a great emphasis placed on higher education. This is why you won't find many professional adult athletes in Singapore – their priority is not on playing sport. Having said that, Singapore is, in fact, bursting with highly competitive developing athletes and their parents. They see success in sport at the youth level as a valuable addition to one's résumé for top academic institutions and a vehicle for scholarship opportunities for universities abroad. The decision to engage the support of a sport psychologist and college facilitators to create a high-performance team around an athlete is taken early for many families.

Opening my own practice has given me the unique experience of continuing my work with young, local talent representing traditional Asian culture. It also allows me to work with expatriate athletes, predominately from the US, Australia and the UK, who live in Singapore and play in their respective international school communities. There is a system in Singapore called Direct School Admission, where students can often get into the top academic high schools in the country based on their sporting merits alone. Many families push their children into sport early to secure these placements. This is particularly the case when the child seems more likely to gain entry through their sporting ability than their academic potential, and they start the kids young.

My Australian colleagues in sport psychology counselling typically work with athletes 15 years and older, with the majority of their clientele between 18 and 21 years of age. These young people are making their mark in the elite ranks. In Singapore, the average age of my clients is around 13 years old, and many are as young as 10 and 11.

The typical cases and prototypes that guide best practice in sport psychology are modelled from the experiences of professional adult athletes. Working as a psychologist for such young athletes just isn't the norm in my profession.

Over the years, I've found myself in the unique and privileged position of studying the mindset, challenges and patterns of young athletes, which at present is not well researched or well understood in sport. In the process, I have felt inspired listening to their stories, and more often than not, discouraged by their challenges and struggles. I have the opportunity to see sport through the eyes of very young athletes, and I am compelled to share my insights with parents, teachers and coaches.

Working with young athletes means working closely with their parents too, learning about their challenges, anxieties and sacrifices in the journey alongside their children. The questions these parents have asked me have created new directions for me in my role. When it comes to being a sport-parent I acknowledge there are not many resources available, and I find the standard advice authorities in sport give to parents is too often generic and patronising, such as, 'Please remember, these are kids', 'It's a game', 'The coaches are volunteers', 'The umpires are human', or 'This is not professional sport.'

It's common for parents to feel unsure about how best to support their young athletes in their sport journey. Typically, they follow a process of trial and error, and pick up a few practices along the way that are reinforced by an elite sport culture. I have listened to their questions and that has led me to write this book.

The challenges and psychological issues I see in young athletes from traditional Asian backgrounds are not distinct from the experiences of young people from around the world. In fact, the cases are very similar. The psychological issues we explore in this book are universal in youth sport, and the techniques and strategies I introduce for parents are transferable across cultures.

The following examples were my initial inspiration for this book. These case studies are not written about one actual person; they cannot be identified as one athlete or individual. They are composite examples that represent specific situations and experiences I have witnessed many times over the years. They are situations that are common in the lives of young athletes across all sports.

Throughout this book I use the term 'young athlete' to refer to any child or teenager between 9 and 15 years of age, who is playing sport at any level. The word 'athlete' is not limited to children or teenagers who are playing at an elite level. You are probably reading this book because you are parent, coach or teacher in a position to support and mentor 'young athletes'. In some places, I use the term 'your child' when we discuss strategies and actions specific to parents reading this book.

You might wonder why I've specified the age range from 9 to 15 years. Why not 12 to 18 years? Let me explain. At any level of sport, there are three distinct transitions young athletes go through from 9 to 15 years of age:

- **9–11 years** – the 'just for fun' stage
- **11–12 years** – the stage when many young athletes transition from 'just for fun' to 'more serious'
- **12–15 years** – the stage most young athletes are 'competing and mastering skills'.

The case studies I present in this book capture these transitions as well as the challenges young athletes face from their perspectives. The strategies I will share can support all young athletes through every stage.

Case 1: Coping with early achievement

Max's swimming coach describes him as scary quick in the pool, oozing talent and a quiet, hard worker in his training sessions. Recently, Max has blown his competitors away in local age-group meets and has everyone talking about his speed.

Max walks into my office and sits down in an armchair facing me, looking down at the floor, with his hands in his lap. He begins to explain why he thinks his mum brought him by for the first session today. Max speaks quietly but quickly.

'I just don't want to go to nationals, and my mum says I don't have to go if I really don't want to, but it would be a shame because I have been doing really well. I don't know what to do, I don't want to let anyone down. I like training and trying my best. I don't like racing. I get so nervous and I hate that feeling. I just want the competition to be over the moment it starts, and most competitions take all day and nationals runs for an entire week. And now it's worse because my friends keep telling me that I am going to win and that I'm going to be the best in my age group. Well, I could be, except for this one boy that's pretty close to me. Now I keep thinking everyone expects me to win, and I am scared I am going to lose, and what will everyone think about me then?'

Within these first few minutes of our meeting, I get a sense of Max's personality, which could be prone to anxiety and self-consciousness. He might be the conscientious type and possibly eager to please others. I can feel the heavy burden of others' expectations and the judgments he perceives his friends and family have made. I learn that this burden wasn't there a few months ago when he was almost in his own world, and said he was 'swimming to swim' and 'training to train'.

You might assume Max's case is about personality and vulnerabilities to certain types of experiences, such as anxiety or fear of failure in the competitive arena. Throughout this book, we will discuss how you can support all these symptoms and prevent them in young high achievers, including perfectionist young athletes. However, that is not the main reason for presenting this example. The main point, and a defining message for me in writing this book, is found in the following statement. It epitomises the perspective of so many talented young athletes who experience the situation represented by Max's case: 'I don't even know how I did well in the first place, it just sort of happened. So what if I was just lucky or something and now everyone expects me to keep doing well?'

There it is, a statement that makes me hold my breath, because it describes a phenomenon that is relevant to the psychology of all young athletes, not just those with certain personal characteristics, but also the most confident and competitive boy or girl. In this statement, the athlete highlights that they simply do not know *how* to compete. They have trained and developed the physical skills ready for racing. However, coaches or parents rarely consider the mental preparation for competition that is necessary for athletes of this age.

Competition as a milestone

When young athletes first start competing, expectations to achieve a certain time, place or score are not set explicitly. Typically, coaches, parents and athletes all approach competition as a milestone or initial benchmark to see where the athlete stands in comparison to their peers. Without the pressure to perform, young athletes perform well on autopilot, relying solely on the body to replicate what it has been doing in training. But it only takes one or two competitive experiences to change the nature of competition. For example, a young swimmer can happily swim up and down the pool in training, humming a song in their head or thinking about what's for dinner that night, with very little consequence to their performance. But when they move to the competitive arena, the focus on hitting times and the impending evaluation from coaches, parents and peers throws them off guard. Mentally managing these new expectations, not to mention the nervousness they feel, requires a totally different type of focus and set of coping skills, compared to the training environment.

A traditional coaching approach to this dilemma would be to suggest that the athlete just needs more experience in the competitive arena. More experience, in the traditional sense, is about becoming familiar with the external environment, the setting and the people. However, gaining experience doesn't guarantee that the athlete will become more aware of what is happening in their mind and body from one competition to the next. Athletes can compete in lots of events, over many seasons, without developing an understanding of what is happening in their minds. Building this type of internal awareness requires training and reflection, and only when this happens can an athlete develop skills to thrive and enjoy competing long-term.

If you have heard similar recommendations that your child 'simply needs more experience competing', then an important question to ask is, 'Experience in what? What is the athlete gaining experience with?'

The two primary experiences the child gains in this 'sink or swim' approach to competing in sport are:

- **Stress inoculation** – Continuous bouts of exposure to the competitive arena that are out of the athlete's comfort zone, and therefore exposure to new feelings of stress and pressure. This is to say, young athletes are gaining experience with the feelings of being stressed out without having the coping strategies to deal with them. Over time they connect that feeling of stress with competing and the competition surroundings.
- **Experience with meeting OR not meeting expectations** – This can be in the form of winning or losing, measuring one's performance against benchmarks or goals set by the parents, coach or the young athletes themselves.

Most parents would agree that through these learning experiences, the child gains valuable and important life lessons. That can be true. However, parents, teachers and coaches need to understand that learning experiences can only occur if you are ready to capture these learnings through systematic debrief and reflections together in positive ways before, during and after the game. Without this step, the child quickly forms their own assumptions about themselves and the competitive arena. These views are rarely positive if they haven't met the athlete's performance expectations.

Another challenging factor to acknowledge in this scenario is that the age of the children participating on highly competitive sports stages is getting younger. Coaches would agree that a decade ago, this transition typically took place around the age of 14–16 years. Today it is not uncommon to see children of 11–13 years with a strong, result-oriented focus in their sport endeavours. The age gap between readiness to compete physically and psychologically has increased. Time spent preparing physically to compete is prioritised at 11–13 years of age but psychological preparation, or even awareness training prior to competitive events, is completely underestimated.

The younger the child is, the more challenging it is for them to self-learn purely by experience. This is because they have not developed skills in positive self-reflection, or coping skills to adapt to the competitive environment. The primary goals of this book are to empower parents, teachers and coaches to facilitate positive reflection processes and awareness training in their young athletes; to close the gap between physical and mental readiness to compete; to prevent performance anxiety; and to raise the possibility for athletes to enjoy themselves and thrive in even the most competitive environments.

The learnings from the experience approach in sport apply not only to children, but also to parents in their supporting roles. Research on parents in sport has revealed that rather than being supported or guided to develop strategies that may help them to cope with demands, parents often develop coping strategies through a process of trial and error and their own experiences in the sport (Burgess et al., 2016). I want this book to provide you with peace of mind and assurance that what you say, think and do will be the optimal way to support your child so you can enjoy the journey together.

Case 2: The transition from 'just for fun' to 'more serious'

Alvin was 11 turning 12 when I met him. He stopped by my office for the first time and sat down in a chair alongside his dad.

'We have just started taking things a bit more seriously with Alvin's sport,' his father said.

Alvin was recruited to join a professional, elite youth football club, playing in both his age division and up a level for U14 matches. Alvin's dad stayed in the room for 10 minutes for a team talk amongst the three of us, which is part of my standard protocol. He explained that Alvin loved football and his dream was to play professionally. Alvin had been in the new club system for six months and he wasn't enjoying his football as much as he used to. He didn't feel as confident as he used to, but it wasn't because he was comparing himself to his teammates. He felt he could play up with them okay, but he wasn't performing as well as he could or had in the past. He often felt indecisive on the pitch, saying to himself, 'Should I run with the ball or cross it?' Alvin's coach said he needed to work on reacting faster.

Then Alvin's dad left so I could continue the session one-to-one with Alvin. When we were on our own, Alvin said to me, 'I don't want to mess up, and you're benched when you make a mistake in matches. After the matches I just keep thinking about the mistakes I made and think, why did I do that? It's so stupid and I hate that feeling. I know it's supposed to help me improve and this team is one of the best in the region, I just don't know if I want to keep playing football. I don't know if I like football anymore. I like it when I play well, but mainly when I don't make mistakes, I feel relieved.'

This example represents the most common psychological challenge I see in young athletes between the age of 11 and 13 years. The transition from 'just for fun' to 'more serious' is a significantly under-researched phenomenon in sport psychology. In this book, I attempt to offer parents some insights into why this transition can be so challenging. I also outline strategies to counter the common negative patterns I witness in young athletes and parental behaviours in this stage of a child's sport journey.

What does more serious mean?

After interviewing many parents and coaches about what 'more serious' actually means, I have noticed one key feature in the learning environment – a focus on skill acquisition and raising the standard of performance by the scrutiny of mistakes.

In transitioning from playing 'just for fun' to playing more competitively, children quickly adopt attitudes and beliefs about errors and performance that align with perfectionist standards in elite sport culture. When we explore this concept in group workshops with young athletes, I use an anonymous polling exercise. I ask athletes how strongly they agree or disagree with the following statements:

- in order to have a great personal performance, I must avoid making errors
- mistakes that cost us the game deserve punishment
- I think about the mistakes I made for a long while after the match has finished

- if I make mistakes early in a match it's a sign it's not going to be a good game for me.

Generally, the younger groups are less likely to agree with these statements. The practices, ideas and messages of coaches and parents that support athletes under 11 years old convey the dominant storyline of having fun and trying new things. Mistakes are accepted and expected.

Interestingly, I have observed a significant jump in the number of athletes in the 11–13 years age group who agree with these statements, in particular, the statement that mistakes should be punishable. In competitive youth football, in this age group, it's a common coaching practice to bench players following a mistake in matches, which reinforces this message. It is clear to me that athletes of 11–13 years of age take these statements seriously and it is part of the dominant storyline in this group's transition from 'just having fun' to becoming a 'serious' competitor.

Across the globe, the youth sports clubs most sought after by parents are those that promote elite development and pathways to the professional ranks. Don't get me wrong, this is a great concept, except that the dominant approach to developing young athletes in this system is through the scrutiny of errors and perfectionist striving to improve competitive performance. As a consequence, the emerging mindset I witness more and more in young athletes is a strong emphasis on avoiding errors. This translates to less confident and overly cautious athletes in the competition arena. There is a tendency to give up once the athlete recognises that a few mistakes have been made. In addition to this, if a child receives criticism for attempting a certain skill, they might deliberately avoid attempts to use that skill in the next match. Debriefing with a primary focus on scrutiny of errors might not necessarily benefit children's development in sport.

This is consistent with findings from research in sport psychology looking into the culture of sport in youth swimming in Australia (McMahon & Penney, 2015). The research explores the topics of performance and perfection pervading the practices and conversations of coaches, parents, athletes and club officials. For example, weekly weigh-ins and strict diet practices emphasise that swimmers' bodies should be managed, monitored and controlled as a means of improving competitive performance. Perfection is pursued through constantly improving technique and correcting weaknesses and mistakes. This was strongly supported by parents' post-race feedback to their swimmers. According to the swimmers, their parents seemingly did this without question, believing that the ideas they were enforcing were 'the only way to be' within Australian swimming culture.

I believe that the pressure on young athletes to strive, compete and meet increasing expectations in both school and sport is a direct reflection of the cultural changes in broader society. Recent research has shown that perfectionist striving is rising over time amongst young people (Curran & Hill, 2019). I have also witnessed a rise in student athletes visiting my clinic due to their perfectionist mindset, and the challenges they face because of it. As young people's expectations have increased, so have the demands placed on them. Intense competition for elite college admission has meant that, relative to previous generations, current high school students must stand out just to be accepted. An increasingly popular strategy to stand out is to become a top student and a top athlete simultaneously by the time one reaches college. This may or may not be the goal you want your child to achieve. But either way, we must acknowledge the cultural shift our children are facing. We might not be able to change the culture, but in your role as a parent, coach or teacher you can equip your young athletes with new and different strategies to better manage and even thrive in an increasingly demanding environment. In Chapter 5, we will look closely at the perfectionist athlete and the perfectionist parent.

The parent trap

When a sports environment emphasises the inspection and analysis of mistakes in young athletes, feedback from parents and coaches gravitates toward pointing out specific errors, while praise actually becomes vaguer. For instance, it's not uncommon to hear a golf parent say, 'Good job today, *but* what happened on the hole when you made a double-bogey?'

What follows in a conversation such as this is a detailed list of mistakes captured with hawk-eye vision similar to the best performance analysts in professional sport. In this environment, how does a young athlete gauge how well or how poorly they performed on a given day? Interestingly, I often hear kids say, 'I know I've performed well when I don't get called out for mistakes I made on the course, and I feel more relaxed.'

Parents are in a position to praise, instruct and critique their children in sport. When this occurs *during* competitive events, such communication is referred to as 'parent verbal sideline behaviour'. Directly *after* the game, during the car ride home, is another point at which parents have great influence over their athlete's relationship with sport. The conversations you engage in with your athlete after the game that critique or offer feedback about their performance, are typically referred to as 'debriefing'. It is the most highly practiced but contentious aspect of parental influence in youth sport.

During and *after* the game are two spaces in which parents have the strongest influence over their child's development in sport. They are also the spaces where parents fall into common traps that negatively impact their child's relationship and the future of their involvement in their sport journey.

You may be keen for your child to simply enjoy their sport and you might have no intention of getting serious on the sidelines. Without realising it, though, you can find yourself quickly and automatically interacting with your child in a way that doesn't align with this desire, and there is research to support this shift.

What is the research telling us?

Researchers Dorsch and colleagues (Dorsch et al., 2015) followed the verbal sideline actions of four first-time youth sport parents involved in a soccer league (two mothers and two fathers) in the Midwest of the United States over the course of five sport seasons. These parents were targeted for the study because they shared the expectation of their children to continue over multiple seasons. The children were five to six years of age at the beginning of the study and the parents had a range of sporting backgrounds, from no formal playing experience to college-level experience. Over the course of five seasons, the number of verbal comments and instructions made by parents from the sideline increased, and parents were more willing to offer negative feedback to their children by season five. One parent commented, 'Over time, when he plays the same sport, over and over again, I guess I have the expectation that he will be learning and picking up a few things as he goes along.'

This transformation in interaction can be influenced by a child's increasing ability and the expectations parents develop quite quickly in the sport. The study did not look at how these changes in parent sideline actions influenced the child and their relationship with their sport. The child's ability is growing exponentially between the ages of six and 12 years old, but can we say the same for their confidence? The cases I see of performance anxiety at the latter age suggests not.

Extrapolating from this research, if we know that parental expectations are rising quickly and negative feedback is also increasing, observations from the sideline are more likely to be focused on identifying errors and discrepancies and commenting on, and correcting, the child's actions. Parents can fall into the common trap of negative sideline behaviours and demoralising post-game debriefs without realising it. As young athletes develop greater skill and learn through experience in their sport, parents expect to witness a downward trend of fewer and fewer errors from one competition to the next. For many parents, this becomes the only thing they attend to when watching from the sidelines. So, it is no wonder that the analysis of mistakes hole-by-hole, or point-by-point, is the central theme in parent–athlete discussions following a competition.

I believe this is a by-product of the aim of striving for perfection that dominates most sport cultures at the elite level, and pervades the dominant messages of coaches and parents in youth sports groups. We should keep in mind that these sports groups are stepping stones to the professional ranks. In turn, the primary focus for these young athletes is to avoid making errors. They will approach their sport with caution, instead of attacking their sport by driving the positive actions that support high performance. This approach, reinforced by our communication and interaction with our children, is creating perfectionist athletes. And not in a good way, but in a way that creates fear, avoidance and anxiety. Instead, we should create an environment that encourages assertive, confident and courageous young athletes.

The current approach to competition debriefing is guided by a belief that the best way to make a young athlete better is to identify errors and offer ways to improve. With this approach, parents, coaches and teachers are missing out on the opportunity to focus on the facts that truly raise performance and confidence. This book will help you create this opportunity more often.

Most parents invested in sport are more aware than ever before of the pressures they can impose on their children and the negative consequences this has on their sport journey together. At the same time, they are unsure about what they should say, do, or think to best support their young athletes. I acknowledge that invested sport parents absolutely want their child to enjoy their sport and reap the rewards from competing long-term at a high level, but there is a disconnect between these goals and the interactions of parents with their children from the sidelines and in the car ride home.

In 2017, renowned researchers in youth sport, Professors Elliot and Drummond, interviewed parents and their children aged 12 to 13 years old involved in junior Australian football (Elliot & Drummond, 2017). Interestingly, all 34 parents who took part in the study agreed that debriefing had the potential to upset children, but felt strongly that it was an important part of their children's development in sport and life. They said that it reflected 'good' sports parenting. Regardless of the good intentions parents believe they have, children interpret verbal comments in post-game debriefing as mostly corrective, critical or negative. This goes against the research, which suggests that children prefer largely positive feedback from parents after competition.

It is easy for parents and coaches alike to get swept up in the dominant practices of sport culture, which is strongly influenced by the practices at the elite level. For instance, it is common for coaches in the professional ranks to hold post-game press conferences and performance-analysis sessions. They typically involve harsh and honest appraisals of team, or individual, performances. Consistent with this practice, Elliott and Drummond's research found that parents favour an honest approach to debriefing. This comment from a parent involved in the study reflects this preference: 'I will call a spade a spade, if I think he played crap, I'll say, "Look mate, you played crap today." He hates it, but later on he'll slowly get over it.'

I am not saying that honesty is bad here. Stating the facts without sugar coating things is important for building trust with your athletes. Young athletes can smell disingenuous praise a mile away, and when this happens often enough, they will deflect more genuine praise in the future. You have to look at honesty and the content of your feedback as a whole.

When the feedback focuses on the scrutiny of errors, an honest critique of a performance can become especially disheartening. I have observed time and time again, athletes as young as eight recount every error they made in their last match with granular detail. Children know when they haven't performed well. When this happens and parental feedback is primarily negative, their feelings of anxiety and dissatisfaction are heightened. If we acknowledge the research that shows fun is the strongest motivator for young athletes, it is crucial we find ways to maintain this as an important component in children's sport. We should make sure our communication helps children thrive in their sport if we want them to sustain the journey to the elite ranks.

In general, the current debriefing practices of coaches and parents teach children that performance quality is more important than playing sport for fun. We need to ask how we can strike a balance between creating teachable moments that offer an honest critique that helps our children grow, and at the same time maintaining an emphasis on playing for fun.

The dominant debriefing styles of coaches and parents reinforce a distinction between *playing* and *performing* in youth sport. Playing and performing do not have to be mutually exclusive and there are strategies that can incorporate both into conversations around your child's sport, as I will discuss in this book. Conversations that move the emphasis away from the critique of errors can still provide honest feedback, encourage high-performance habits, and build your child's confidence and enjoyment in their Performance Process.

Changing some of the more negative practices within the culture of youth sport will take time. Some traditional practices and coaching styles in sport are so ingrained they might always remain in some way, shape or form. It will help to be aware of them and to be prepared to question their purpose.

Parent goals

Parent verbal sideline behaviour is greatly influenced by the goals you have for you child in their sport. We must look beyond the goals that simply focus on the results, outcomes and achievements, and consciously connect with the hopes and desires you have for your child in their sport endeavours.

Think about your initial reasons for signing your child up in their sport. What did you hope would be a result of your child's involvement in sport? You will find that these hopes and desires for your child are connected to your values and what matters most to you as a parent.

The research has found three central themes to categorise parents' goals for their children in youth sport (Dorsch et al., 2015).

1. **Development and learning goals:** centred on developing as an athlete and growing as an individual, such as improving technical skills, learning to work hard, or preparing for a scholarship.
2. **Identity goals:** the athlete projecting a good image or reputation, such as showing a good attitude, comparing well to other athletes, or avoiding other parents' negative views.
3. **Relationship goals:** enhancing family relationships or building relationships with others, such as spending time together, feeling supported by the family, learning sportsmanship and teamwork.

This exercise will help you gain clarity about the multiple goals you have for your child in their sport. It will help to direct your sideline comments and post-game feedback in ways that align with these goals and your values.

Example: parent goal sheet for a young male golfer

Development Goals	• For my son to become more confident in himself and unafraid of taking risks, play risky shots and try new things, learn creativity with his short-game. • For my son to gain fighting spirit, like learning to keep trying and not give up when playing poorly and learning to manage his emotions well and to stay calm and positive after a double-bogey or a three-putt. • For my son to learn decision making skills through course management. • For my son to be happy and have fun.
Identity Goals	• For my son to become a playing partner that other kids and adults want to play with – say 'good shot' with genuine feeling and help others look for their ball. • For my son to be a fair competitor and always respect his playing partners, officials and the rules of golf.
Relationship Goals	• To encourage and support my son's goals and dreams, not force my own expectations and desires onto him. • To create open communication to discuss my son's coaching preferences, decisions with swing changes, and his feelings about competing. • To ensure we have quality family time, building a weekend ritual of playing a round or going to the range as a family and having a meal together afterward. • To allow my son to develop a good relationship with his coach, and I will stay out of it unless he brings it up, or I see he is unhappy.

In the space below, record the goals you have for your child in their sport at this time.

Development Goals	
Identity Goals	
Relationship Goals	

Dorsh and colleagues observed parents' use of 'editing' to deal with goal conflict. For example, parents choose not to say negative comments loud enough for their children to hear, or comment to another parent close by instead of talking directly to the child. Watching your child participate in sport can be an emotional experience, which can escalate as you invest more time and money into your child's development in sport. There are many factors that can intensify your emotions on the sidelines and trigger behaviours and reactions that greatly affect your child. Parents experience anger in situations when behaviours of the coach, referee, athletes or other parents are perceived to be unjust, uncaring or incompetent. What's more, I understand deeply the growing levels of stress and obligation parents can feel as their child progresses in their sport, especially if they have been told their child is talented.

It is both exciting and stressful to feel your time and financial demands increase alongside your athlete's development. Once the game is in motion, emotions run high, and the knee-jerk reaction can be to shout instructions, 'What was that? Come on, focus!'

After the game, emotions can also take over, and I have listened to regretful parents describe their comments and reactions, such as 'I know I shouldn't have said it, but I felt angry that he performed so badly in his last competition, like he didn't even try. So I said to him, "Why am I sacrificing so much for you, all the family's money to give you the chance to become a professional one day and this is how you act? If you keep this up, I am not going to invest in this anymore, you can just do this recreationally and that's it."'

It is hard to take comments like this back, and they do, unfortunately, influence a child's experience of pressure to perform. You might need to put a strategy in place to stop yourself from doing this. Keep in mind that certain goals you have for your child can be helpful for you too. Relationship goals, in particular, work well, such as bonding with your child, or wanting your child to feel supported by the family. Relationship goals can lead parents and coaches to prioritise communication that enhances feelings of closeness with their children. At the conclusion of the game, prioritising your relationship goals can help you respond in encouraging and supportive ways and refrain from being emotionally reactive.

To master these key moments, we will look specifically at the feedback process in Chapter 4, where I provide tools and techniques to build a positive and collaborative reflection process.

Case 3: Teen athlete transitioning from sub-elite to elite ranks

Priya is 15 and has just begun home schooling to dedicate more time to tennis. She travels almost every week to a different tournament. Lately she has let her emotions get the better of her on court.

'I've been feeling great in training and I know I'm close to having some break-out matches, but it's not coming out. I get frustrated and rather than taking my time to build the rally, I try to close it out quickly and go for winners. Then I hit it out and lose the point, and I just spiral down from there. I am training so much because I think I'm expected to win and play better, and everyone thinks I should be a much better player. Now that I'm home schooling I feel more pressure to play well, and I feel worse when I lose. My parents are spending so much money on me and have invested so much, I should be winning more matches.'

Parent pride

One of the things I discuss with athletes with similar dilemmas to Priya's is the re-evaluation of what makes their parents proud of them in their sport journey. I start with the question, 'What makes your mum and dad proud, even when you lose matches?'

Generally speaking, invested parents with some sport knowledge do not expect their child to win *all* the time. What they do expect is a good attitude, sustaining a high level of effort throughout the match, and not giving up when they're behind. Very often the child heaves a sigh of relief when we talk about the attributes that make their parent proud, even when the child loses a match. It's as if the child thinks, This is so logical, I know this, but somehow I completely forgot about it.

Often athletes in this position will agree with me and, smiling, they say, 'Oh yeah, that's pretty true actually, but now I think about the matches I have lost recently and it was because I tanked.' They realise that solely focusing on the results they want to achieve doesn't win matches. In order to compete well consistently, athletes must also focus on developing and executing professional habits, such as self-control and bouncing back from errors. Most athletes negotiating the leap from amateur to elite ranks do not prioritise these skills in training or competition. Being professional is about forming professional habits; what follows with deliberate effort over time is a new performance standard.

Many young athletes who are transitioning to elite groups, or have just turned professional, develop a results-only focus. When I ask athletes who are in a similar position to Priya about what it means to be professional, they say it means error-free performances, constantly perfecting their technique, high consistency and accuracy.

From my perspective, instead of these perfectionist expectations coming to the fore at this stage in their sport journey, a stronger emphasis on professional habits is actually required. This includes managing emotions and focus, and being rational and resilient in the face of errors and setbacks. Unfortunately, instead of further developing or refining the skills that facilitate top performance, this aspect is often left in the background. The dominant attitude is that these habits should be there already, somehow ingrained in the athlete.

I observe that these habits are rarely emphasised in training or matches, or included systematically in post-match debriefs. Nor are they individually prioritised in goal-setting and development plans. As a result, athletes transitioning to the professional ranks place little importance on the use of these important habits that support high performance. The case of Priya represents a common pattern I see in most athletes at this stage in their career. They march out onto the court or field with high expectations, ready to demonstrate their technical prowess, expecting to hit perfect shots and intending to make as few errors as possible. But the intention to manage emotions or reactions to errors, along with consistent routines and the ability to refocus effectively between points, is not at the forefront of their mind going into the match (because this is a given, right?).

What happens with this imbalance is that as soon as the flaws begin to show, emotions rise quickly, attitude and body language drop, and the moment the possibility of winning seems doubtful, the athlete will tank; in other words, give up on the match. They will revert to a pattern of actions in the arena that is considered to be unacceptable behaviour, such as emotional outbursts that result in penalties or disqualification. They end up looking immature, like someone with a big ego and a bad attitude. Far from the professional that people tell them they could be. Many athletes in this transition to the professional ranks feel that their playing is worse than before they started to train for significantly more hours. This can be unsettling, because the usual advice to 'train harder' suddenly doesn't seem to apply. I believe it is the imbalance between performance expectations and expectations placed on professional habits that is creating this dilemma.

One way to view this issue is that the value and importance placed on striving for perfection, error-free performance and good results is greater than the value placed on the actions or habits that support high performance. These latter traits sit inside the category I call the 'Performance Process'. You cannot achieve high standards and lofty goals without placing a high value and emphasis on this aspect.

The Performance Process

The Performance Process involves all the mental and physical habits the athlete *performs* in training and competition that lead to particular outcomes. These habits are like *ingredients* in baking the ultimate cake for peak performance. The list of ingredients in this recipe can become very detailed and specific to the sport as your child develops to the elite level. Below is a general list of the base ingredients or habits for building a strong foundation. These things shouldn't really change in importance from sub-elite to elite in your child's development in their sport. They should remain all-important.

Base ingredients include:

- effort
- positive self-talk
- positive reaction to mistakes
- post-game reflections that support confidence and motivation
- discipline in the form of focusing in the present and managing distractions
- pre-game rituals to activate the mind and body.

Coaches and athletes at the top level would describe these habits as the 'little' things that make the difference. I prefer to talk about them as the 'big ticket items' that matter the most.

As you read through the list, you might be thinking, yes I know this, I value the process. But what you need to be thinking about is your athlete's focus and values. When your child approaches 11 and 12 years of age and moves to competing competitively, they fall into a results-only focus very quickly.

The ingredients I have listed in the process are not even a blip on their radar. Up to this point, your child has been repeatedly praised primarily for their results, times and scores. To add to that, the results come quite easily when they are younger. Your athlete is not aware of the key habits in the process as much as you may think they are. This is the transitional phase when there's a sudden and increasing emphasis placed on attaining certain results by you – the parents, coaches and teachers. And yet, the child does not have a solid awareness of the habits that actually help to direct and achieve high performance. At this point, it is critical that your athlete learns to look into the key habits in their Performance Process and learns to value the process, just as much as the results. To facilitate this step, you need to emphasise the process before, during and after the game. In this book, I will show you how.

When an athlete has low expectations in the Performance Process, it means they don't take much care of these habits. They are an after-thought. Activities or discussions to develop these habits are not integrated into training. Strategies to engage these habits in the competitive environment are not prioritised in the mind of the athlete before or during the match. Instead, most athletes will solely focus on the technical or tactical approach for the match. In reflections following a match, I frequently see athletes and coaches highlighting one of the factors in the list above (e.g., emotional control), to be the *primary* cause of their loss or down-slide in performance, but it is rarely set-up proactively as a priority to take care of during the match.

Separating the Performance Process from the results, here is a list of the various outcomes that generally fit into the results space of your child's sport:

- winning OR not losing
- PBs (new personal bests)
- specific times or scores
- place or medal
- rankings.

One of the most important points to understand in your supporting role is the degree of control your athlete has over these components when training and competing. The Performance Process is highly controllable. As your child learns skills to develop, refine and control activation of the habits in the Performance Process, they are 100% accountable for *performing* these actions when competing. The results are a different matter. Your child has a low degree of control over the results and outcomes. When competing, the result is a future-factor, and your child can only truly control what exists in the present moment (i.e., their thoughts, feelings and actions in the Performance Process). The desired result is not a given, even if your athlete is training well or competing against a less-experienced opponent.

The message here is that a desired result isn't something that 'should be' or 'should happen', or described as an *expectation*. When parents and athletes have high expectations for the results, without much consideration of their Performance Process, it can be called a results-only focus. The athlete will think about the results they want to achieve for days or weeks in advance, but usually not in a way that creates excitement or confidence about the event. The athlete with a results-only focus will feel pressure and anxiety, because the degree of control over the results is low. They run through *what-if* scenarios about winning and losing. Their thoughts gravitate toward hoping they will perform well, hoping they won't lose, and trying not to lose in their performance.

Athletes can perform well under pressure, but only if they have strong anchors in their process that effectively draw their attention away from the nerve-racking feeling in their body and the possible outcomes of the game. Anchors help them feel immersed in the task at hand, and feel the flow in their skill execution, just as they have trained.

Process vs results

In our conversations about performance with our athletes, we need to place equal importance on the results and the Performance Process. To establish the value and importance of the Performance Process, we need to make it tangible. We have to see it and feel it and it bring to life. But often the ingredients in this system are not obvious until we start to talk about them more, think about them more, and look for them when a child is competing. When you watch your child from the sidelines, the natural tendency is to observe with no real intent in mind, and you notice the mistakes or less optimal actions first. This approach feels valuable because our brains pick up on the errors easily; you feel engaged because you can provide specific and immediate feedback in the form of instructions to correct the errors, or encouragement to show your support.

In the table following, write down the professional habits that sit inside the Performance Process you value in your child's development in their sport. Focus on the actions; the things you can see. It is easy to gravitate toward listing qualities such as determination and work ethic. Characteristics such as these are related, but they are harder to see, so write down the actual action or habit that you want to see the athlete demonstrate on the pitch.

In the second column, describe what you would see if you were to watch out for this habit from the sidelines; what you would observe them doing. Think of a recent scenario when you witnessed your child showing this habit really well. Don't worry if you find it hard to describe these actions; from my experience, most parents find it challenging at first. Instead of trying this exercise on your own, it can be valuable to build this chart with your athlete. You might be surprised by their level of input, especially when it comes to translating the habits you value into actions you can see from the sidelines.

This is the first step in building your awareness around the habits and behaviours that you both value greatly in sport. Developing some of these habits might be why you wanted your child to be involved in sport in the first place.

By the end of this book, you will know the habits and behaviours that are linked to high performance in your child's sport in great detail. When you have a clear picture of what these habits look like in your child's sport, you will be better able to watch out for them when observing your child perform – you'll notice more than just the errors and the results. Knowing what to look out for, and being prepared to provide specific feedback about these positive behaviours following every competition, will bring to the fore just how important these habits are in directing performance, in both your mind and your child's moving forward.

Bringing awareness to the original goals you have for your child and the actions you value in their sport can prevent you from getting swept up automatically in the dominant practice of your child's sport, which is not always positive. Consider the exercises in this chapter as a way to break that circuit and stick to positive habits and communication styles that reinforce your true goals and values in your child's sport.

Chapter 2 sets the tone for creating conversations in casual or structured ways with your athlete that will kickstart a pure focus on the Performance Process. In Chapters 3 and 4, I introduce tools and techniques for debriefing that will incorporate the information you generate below.

There is no one-size-fits-all approach, or a perfect set of habits for all sports. There are habits that are important for high performance across sports and cultures, but ultimately, the habits you select can be guided by your personal views. Your responses may also be influenced by the messages and values emphasised in your child's sports club or school.

Habits in the Performance Process

Example in soccer/football

The habits you value most in your child's sport development	Now describe what this looks like, as if you were watching through the lens of a camera, what you would see if they demonstrated this habit when competing
Effort never giving up	Running bursts, or chasing down the ball. Running hard throughout the match regardless of the score, most notably when behind in a match. Maintaining loud, positive and precise instructions or encouragement to teammates from the start of the match to the finish – regardless of score, most notably when losing or behind in the match.
Resilience bouncing back from mistakes or set-backs	A deep breath between plays, shaking the body out, eyes up, head up. A running burst or chasing down the ball immediately after an error or interception, instead of stopping, gesturing or negative comments directed at self or teammates. Showing patience after a mistake or interception. Containing the attacker, not diving in.
Focus concentration in the present moment and on the task at hand	Looking switched on. Eyes on the play (scanning), moving quickly, sideways on, moving into position early (good position sense and anticipating).

Positivity positive self-talk	Verbal self-encouragement, positive gestures to show positive self-talk is present (e.g., fist pump, clapping, tap on the leg).
Collaboration encouraging teammates	Positive gestures or verbal comments (e.g., calling out to a teammate by name, making eye contact, a tap on a teammate's shoulder, fist pump, clapping or high-five).
Routines maintaining consistency	On the bench subbing in. Stretching, eyes on game, taking deep breaths, staying active, not just sitting there.
Body language positive body language and presentation habits	Eyes up, head up, hands off hips, bouncing on toes, staying active between plays, not standing still.
Feedback receptive to feedback and respect for the coach or other authoritative figures	Nodding to the coach's instructions, open body language and eye contact. Asking questions. Executing the coach's instructions and attempting the corrections immediately.

Example in swimming

The habits you value most in your child's sport development	Now describe what this looks like, as if you were watching through the lens of a camera, what you would see if they demonstrated this habit when competing
Strong start starting strong and assertive in a race	Exploding off the blocks. In the race. Head down, not watching or following other lanes.
Resilience bouncing back from mistakes or set-backs	Moving on quickly after a race – listening to music, eating, talking with friends in the stands, looking forward to the next race – showing positive body language around the pool.
Collaboration encouraging club mates	A positive gesture (or verbal comment directly after a club mate's race). Cheering on a club mate from the stands.
Consistent routines	In the stands, putting on a tracksuit and staying warm, eating, listening to music. In the marshalling area, stretching the arms, neck, rounding the shoulders, taking deep breaths, smiling. For some, talking and laughing. For others, taking a quiet moment for themselves and looking relaxed.
Body language positive body language and presentation habits	At the blocks, taking a deep breath, shaking out body, power pose, slapping the legs, a strong jump or two. For some, a wave to the stands, smiling. For others, eyes straight down the lane, slight adjustment to the goggles.

Feedback receptive to feedback and respect for the coach or other authoritative figures	Approaching the coach after a race. Nodding to the coach's instructions, open body language and eye contact.

Performance Process worksheet

The habits you value most in your child's sport development	Now describe what this looks like, as if you were watching through the lens of a camera, what you would see if they demonstrated this habit when competing
Effort never giving up	
Resilience bouncing back from mistakes or set-backs	
Focus concentration in the present moment and on the task at hand	

Positivity positive self-talk	
Collaboration encouraging teammates	
Routines maintaining consistency	
Body language positive body language and presentation habits	
Feedback receptive to feedback and respect for the coach or other authoritative figures	

QUICK POINTS

- The athlete with a results-only focus will feel pressure and anxiety because the degree of control here is low.
- Don't expect results – aim, strive and chase for results. A desired result isn't something that 'should be' or 'should happen'. Results should not be described as expectations.
- You can build expectations around the process, and high expectations for that matter. Focus more on developing and valuing the key habits in their Performance Process. This is the secret to reducing anxiety and shaping an adaptable athlete.

CHAPTER TWO
THE PROCESS

'I *do* tell him to focus on the process and not the end result.'

'I always say, take it one shot at a time/one point at a time/ one skill at a time.'

These are the messages dedicated sport parents and coaches are reinforcing before every match, game or race. Most of us in a supporting role understand that the general message to our athletes should be to focus more on the process and less on the result when competing. However, the question is, what actually is 'the process' and how do you communicate it to your child?

The process isn't just one thing. It is a combination of thoughts, focus, emotions and actions occurring simultaneously. It can seem obscure, complex and different from one individual to the next, even in the same sport. So where do you start?

Developing an understanding of the process and the ability to follow this process when competing isn't about teaching skills as much as it is about building awareness. One of the primary inspirations for this book came from the collaborative work I have done with young athletes to understand, from their perspective, the process of performance in finer detail.

I am in a privileged position to receive insights about young athletes' experiences in sport that they don't always share openly, or in such detail, with their parents. A deeper understanding of what's happening in your athlete's mind, their emotions and actions in the competitive environment, will shape the building blocks for the following chapters. We will explore strategies for communication before the game and debriefing after the game that will help your child thrive and protect your relationship with them along their sport journey.

Mapping a Process: The Key Ingredients

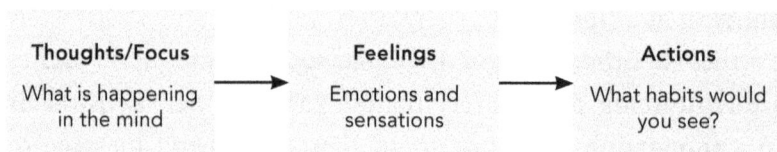

Thoughts/Focus		Feelings		Actions
What is happening in the mind	→	Emotions and sensations	→	What habits would you see?

How I map a process

To understand how to help your athlete focus on the process, you have to learn from their perspective. What they are focused on or thinking about? What do they feel? What actions crop up when they believe they are performing at their best? And their worst? This is how I map a process. In a nutshell, it is the interconnections between an athlete's thoughts, feelings and actions when competing. The core elements are simple, but the details are always intriguing. Over the past 10 years, I have mapped a process that captures the highs and lows of competing from the young athlete's perspective, and I will share valuable insights with you in this chapter.

I refer to the low moments or the experience of sub-optimal performance as the Red Zone, and the high points or experience of peak performance as the Green Zone.

Colour coding allows the brain to organise and group together large amounts of information, enhancing our ability to recognise and respond to a variety of factors quickly when they are presented. In the fast-paced world of sport, being able to recognise Red Zone signals in the form of thoughts, feelings or behaviour, and shift momentum quickly, is crucial in effectively directing performance play by play, or point by point.

A closer look at the Red Zone and Green Zone

The Red Zone leads to poor performance. In this zone, athletes experience negative emotions, and their thoughts and actions are ineffective. The term 'seeing red' is used to describe the psychological state of being frustrated or annoyed, and this is similar to what athletes experience in their Red Zone.

In contrast, the Green Zone leads to peak performance. In this zone, athletes experience positive emotions, and their thoughts and actions are productive. The colour green is symbolic of driving a racing car with your foot on the pedal – you keep moving forward, there is nothing holding you back, and you feel invincible.

In this chapter I share the Red Zone and Green Zone charts that represent the most common thoughts, feelings and actions reported by the young athletes who have worked with me. This information is a summary of 150 young athletes' experiences, aged between 9 and 20 years old (average age = 13 to 14 years old). They were competing in various sports including swimming, tennis, golf, gymnastics, football/soccer, rugby, fencing, badminton, table tennis and ice-skating. I do not map the specific results or score in these two zones. Rather, I am more interested in understanding the process inside each zone, such as the interconnection of thoughts, emotions and actions in the athlete's experience. The athlete might touch on the score as a reference point as we talk through their zone experience, but it is not a focal point of the analysis.

The Red Zone

Table 1: A Red Zone chart representing the most common patterns of thoughts, feelings and actions of 150 young athletes competing in various sports including swimming, tennis, golf, gymnastics, football/soccer, rugby, fencing, badminton, table tennis and ice-skating. The boxes around the table provide a narrative and my analysis of the information in the chart.

The what ifs ... Thinking about negative possibilities →

Unproductive reflection of mistakes →

Attention is shifting between internal and external factors →

Thoughts/ Focus	Feelings	Actions
What if I don't play well? Don't mess this up	Scared Anxious Frustrated Annoyed	Rushing Hesitant and cautious with my movements
When I make a mistake I think, Why did I do that? What am I doing wrong? Should I do this, or that?		Changing things about my technique Blaming my opponent, my team-mates, my equipment, the referee
Focused on how I feel Distracted – noticing the crowd, my parents and my coaches' expressions		Looking around a lot – at the sky, the spectators, my coach, my parents

Trying to find control

Actions that express the feeling of spiralling out of control

At first glance of the Red Zone chart, you may notice lots of questioning and doubting in the Thoughts/Focus column. When coaches and parents share their perspectives on this process, I often hear them say, 'It's a lot of over-thinking, or over-analysing.' This conclusion is understandable. However, I don't believe there is such a thing as the ability to over-think, but rather in this zone, the athlete's focus is directed inward, as if there is a spotlight on their thoughts. They are not focused on the task at hand, but rather focused on the past (on thoughts about mistakes moments ago), or on the future (worrying about negative outcomes).

Interestingly, athletes report more internal dialogue and self-talk in the Red Zone (compared to the Green Zone), predominately in the form of questions, such as, 'What if?', usually about the negative possibilities (e.g., 'What if I perform badly?') or 'Why?' questions, about the mistakes they are making (e.g., 'Why did I do that?'). It may appear as analysis or self-assessment towards problem-solving, but 99% of the time, the young athletes do not have answers for these questions. So, it's not a real assessment at all, only an internal response or reaction to errors that perpetuate negative emotions experienced in the form of frustration or disappointment.

This unproductive style of thinking keeps the athlete focused solely on the problems at hand, such as a potential glitch in their technique or simply what isn't working. As a consequence, they are not directing their performance with instructions or cues that change their actions in helpful ways. This results in feeling stuck and losing control. There is nothing anchoring or grounding the athlete's focus when their thoughts become increasingly reactive to what their opponent is doing, or to a string of errors. Therefore, as their attention broadens, so does the visual focus, increasing the athlete's vulnerability to distractions elsewhere in the environment. For example, tuning in to their parents' expressions in the crowd, the referee or umpire's and their teammates' gestures. This is what it really means to 'lose focus'.

The Red and Green Zone charts are a summation of what young athletes commonly experience across a variety of sports. However, there are specific nuances I have observed in specific sports. In the following sections, I shed light on the distinct patterns I see occurring in select sports such as the performing arts, golf and swimming.

As you read the next section you may find yourself asking, 'What are the solutions to these experiences in the Red Zone?' and 'How do we fix them?' Be patient, solutions will present themselves and you will find them in the Green Zone analysis. The Green Zone provides the key ingredients and anchors for peak performance.

The Red Zone for performing artists

In the performing arts, such as gymnastics, dance and figure skating, where an emphasis is placed on precision in execution and striving for perfection in performance, thoughts in the Red Zone are predominately centred on trying to avoid errors. Thoughts that represent 'Don't mess this up', are typically verbalised by gymnasts and figure skaters as things like 'Don't drop the apparatus', 'I must not fall', and 'I have to land my jumps.' These directly correspond to feelings of anxiousness and tension. Instinctively, the performing artist will try to gain control by exercising more caution in their execution, resulting in tentative movements that gymnasts describe as 'not going for it'. Automaticity is lost and conscious and deliberate focus on the motor skills is elevated. When the athlete adds a feeling of anxiousness to the mix, it leads to the experience known as 'paralysis by analysis'. Young gymnasts describe this as being stuck or frozen in mind and body, standing still on the beam and unable move, forgetting their routine, or finding that suddenly they can falter on basic moves they mastered years ago.

The Red Zone for golfers

In highly technical, closed skill sports such as golf, the phenomenon of 'paralysis by analysis' is also a common experience in the Red Zone. 'What if' questions that represent a focus on negative outcomes (e.g., 'What if I don't play well today?'), and attempts to avoid mistakes (e.g., 'Don't hit it left'), put a spotlight on trying to find the right feeling in one's technique or finding one's swing. A common Red Zone action in response to this type of thinking is to tinker with, or make small adjustments to, one's technique following any shot that doesn't have the desired outcome. For example, changing the grip, set-up, backswing, or feeling at impact on almost every shot in the Red Zone. The focus is pulled away from important external factors, such as the target or the best place to miss, and instead directed inward toward finding the 'right' feeling in one's swing. In ways that are similar to performing artists, self-consciousness is raised and the automaticity of foundational movements is lost, resulting in paralysis by analysis. Junior golfers tell me that when this happens, they can't get comfortable over the ball, their glove doesn't fit right on their hand, and they even feel as if they will forget how to hit the ball.

The Red Zone for swimmers

When preparing for a race, young swimmers' thoughts are naturally results focused, gravitating to hitting a certain time and usually a personal best (PB) in every meet. In the Red Zone, a focus on negative possibilities is reflected in questions such as, 'What if I don't swim well today or get a PB?' If confidence is particularly low, questions such as, 'What if I come last?' come to mind, and the focus gravitates toward trying not to perform worse than others, rather than out-performing others. Not surprisingly, these thoughts lead to anxiousness, tension and shakiness in the body. Comparisons to others that minimise one's potential and maximise that of others is a common corresponding action. Many young swimmers describe this in terms of snap judgments of their competitors on deck. 'I am so nervous, but those swimmers look so confident, they must be better than me.' Once in the pool, anxiety for younger swimmers translates into thrashing at the water or adopting an inefficient stroke, and breathing more frequently. For more experienced junior swimmers, I observe tighter, more controlled movements in their Red Zone profile. The heightened focus on competitors dictates their race execution, trying to follow the pace of other swimmers, and giving up on the race as soon as they fall behind.

Reading these specific accounts, you might think that this sounds similar to what elite athletes might experience in their

Red Zones. That's true, and a primary goal for this chapter is to highlight this point. One of the biggest surprises of my early work, when charting the performance profiles of athletes as young as eight, was how similar their performance states were to elite athletes I worked with; and how rich in detail were their descriptions of these experiences with specific thoughts, feelings and actions. Every time I have an opportunity to sit down for the first time with a junior, I am intrigued to observe their perspective. I'm often surprised, and almost always inspired, by how they see things. Coaches and parents can be quick to assume their athletes are too young for sport psychology training; they should start once they have more experience. Training the mind starts with building awareness, and it's already here to tap into and build upon when the child begins to play sport.

The Green Zone

The Green Zone is synonymous with what Professor Mihaly Csikszentmihalyi first described as a flow state or 'the Zone' (Csikszentmihalyi, 1990). In the Green Zone, an athlete feels as if time has slowed down; there is a sense of clarity and heightened focus; they are immersed in the present moment and in complete control of their movements, skills and execution. Interestingly, the way a young athlete aged 9 to 15 years of age describes elements of their Green Zone, or flow state, is remarkably similar to how elite or professional adult athletes describe it. Of course, the level to which these athletes perform, and what we see if we watch them, differs greatly in skill and maturity. What this tells us, at the experiential level, is that there is something natural and instinctual about 'the Zone' that athletes can tap into from a much younger age than you might expect. Traditional coaching says we should wait for the child to gain 'experience and skill' before we 'teach' them such things as 'the Zone'. This isn't about teaching; it's about tapping into their experience. If they have experience competing, they will recognise performance states in profound and intuitive ways from a much younger age than most adults realise.

A defining feature of the Green Zone and one that is particularly problematic, is the perceived absence of thinking or analysis in this zone. I hear athletes say, 'I'm not thinking about anything really', and it can be challenging to draw out specific thoughts. This feature is what makes the Green Zone, or flow state, elusive and even more challenging to voluntarily replicate. In essence, athletes feel as though 'It just happens!' When you are in the zone you know it, but how you got there, and how you can stay there, seem mysterious. It is because of this phenomenon that it is so important to find ways to build your child's connection to exactly what is happening from their perspective when they are performing well. The Green Zone chart offers a unique but simple way to capture these points. It can be used following any competitive experience.

Table 2: A Green Zone chart representing the most common patterns of thoughts, feelings and actions of 150 young athletes competing in various sports including swimming, tennis, golf, gymnastics, football/soccer, rugby, fencing, badminton, table tennis and ice-skating. The boxes around the table provide a narrative and my analysis of the information in the chart.

Thoughts/Focus	Feelings	Actions
Not a lot of thought. I don't say much to myself	Mind feels clear Relaxed and loose	Chasing after the ball. More aggressive. Going for it
I am clear about what I want to do on the next point/shot/play	Having fun	I take my time (before closed skills). Staying active not passive between points (shaking out body, bouncing on feet)
When I make a mistake, it doesn't matter. I focus on the next point/shot/play		

In the moment, focused on the task at hand →

Focus is external Eyes on the target →

Positive reaction to mistakes →

The physical expression of what coaches describe as 'feeling more free'

In the Green Zone, the athlete is immersed in the task at hand, which is experienced as a strong focus or a connection to the target or the ball. As you can see in the Thoughts/Focus column in Table 2, the athlete highlights perceived clarity in their plan for the next point, shot or play. The corresponding feelings and actions exemplify what coaches describe as playing more freely. When we consider broad distinctions in the Green Zone across sports, there are few. Whether it is a swimmer, golfer, gymnast or football player, the defining features of a present focus, free from worries and expectations on the outcome, and actions that look effortless and assertive, co-exist across sports.

If you want to help your athlete to focus on the process, then facilitating awareness of their Green Zone is the most important place to start. The Green Zone is comprised of all their best ingredients that lead to peak performance. The thoughts, feelings and actions in their Green Zone are reasons to trust. If they attempt to activate even one thought or one action in their Green Zone profile from the beginning of their performance, the likelihood of them feeling the way they want to and building momentum in positive ways is greatly increased.

An athlete can also use their Green Zone ingredients to shift out of the Red Zone. When they notice they are engaging in Red Zone thinking or actions, they can use a simple Green Zone thought or action to change the momentum quickly, from one point to the next. Almost like shifting gears, it can draw them away from the Red Zone process and back into the Green. Knowing this is possible is one of the most powerful learnings for young athletes as it teaches them that they can take control of the thoughts and actions that direct performance. They don't have to wait for the turn onto the back nine-holes to create the circuit breaker, the next set, or the half-time; they can take it into their own hands, moment by moment.

This awareness of the zones can greatly reduce performance anxiety for young athletes, as they understand that no matter what happens, even after a poor start, or multiple errors, they can shift what's happening in simple ways they can control.

The Orange Zone

In our initial sessions, I stick to building the young athlete's awareness of the polarized Red and Green Zones. However, in saying that, there is a zone in between the Red and Green that I refer to as the Orange or Amber Zone. Athletes can gradually recognise this distinction as their self-awareness grows.

The Orange Zone is comprised of the most subtle signals that let the athlete know they are bordering on the Red Zone – on the edge. If they can tune in and recognise the signs quickly, this zone can act as a buffer, signalling to them to slow down, step back, or change the momentum quickly before they see *red*. The awareness of the subtle Orange Zone happens in an organic way once an athlete is aware of and understands their Red and Green Zones. In follow-up sessions, without much prompting, young athletes can pinpoint what's happening in between. I take this as a reminder that self-awareness building is in fact about layering and developing. The athlete must be patient and categorical; cramming will only interfere with their progress.

Table 3 summarises a common Orange Zone experience.

Table 3: An Orange Zone chart representing the most common patterns of thoughts, feelings and actions of 150 young athletes competing in various sports including swimming, tennis, golf, gymnastics, football/soccer, rugby, fencing, badminton, table tennis and ice-skating.

Thoughts/ Focus	Feelings	Actions
Future thinking / looking ahead / thinking about the result or holding the trophy Calculating or predicting the outcome – trying to control the outcome	Tense On edge – antsy Tight	Playing defensively, overly safe and cautious Moving less, more passive Start to rush execution

A shift in focus from the task at hand to the score and end result

Subtle change in game approach and rhythm

When an athlete moves from a Green Zone to an Orange Zone, I typically see a subtle shift in focus away from the present moment, shot or play, towards the score or trying to score. In this instance, the athlete recognises their state of play, forming a narrative in their mind about events to come and finishing well or winning. The self-talk example, 'If I just do this, I can maintain my position', is typical of an Orange Zone focus. It is fixed on protecting the score or maintaining the current position. The most common feeling in this case is tension, and the associated response is to play more defensively and with more control. If the athlete continues in this pattern, they will suddenly move into a Red Zone state, where protecting the score becomes more about avoiding mistakes, and negative reactions to errors become intensified.

Bounce-back ability in the Green Zone

One of the most striking contrasts between the Red Zone and Green Zone profiles in Tables 1 and 2 is the distinct reaction to mistakes. In the Red Zone (Table 1), the inner dialogue and focus of the athlete in response to errors is destructive to performance. The young athlete is primarily focused on negative possibilities, which creates an avoidance approach to their game. This is typically expressed in self-talk with a lot of don'ts instead of dos, intensifying the importance of not making errors. Naturally, trying not to mess up corresponds to cautious movements and hesitation, or making small continuous adjustments to one's technique. Many athletes believe they are responding productively to errors by asking themselves, 'Why did I do that?' or 'What am I doing wrong?' But as I highlighted earlier in the chapter, they rarely come up with an answer to these questions, typically staying stuck in this analysis. At best this line of thinking prompts what not to do on the next shot and the pattern of avoidance continues.

In the Green Zone (Table 2), the inner dialogue and focus of the athlete in response to mistakes is highly productive. The athlete nullifies the mistake in self-talk saying, 'It's okay'; they do not dwell on the error, let it go by, and focus their attention on the next move, point or skill. If we assess the flow-on effect from thoughts, feelings and actions in the Green Zone, we can argue that it is not necessarily the absence of errors that contributes most significantly to optimal Performance Process. Rather, it is the positive response to errors that maintains a focus on the task at hand and protects against the compounding of errors as the game progresses.

So, why is the reaction to mistakes so positive in the Green Zone and distinctly counterproductive in the Red? It is easy to conclude that it must have something to do with the underlying score. Perhaps the athlete is more confident in their position to win and therefore less concerned about errors.

First, if this were true, we would see a focus on the score or position more distinctly in the Thoughts/Focus column in the Green Zone chart. Second, if we revisit the profile of the Orange Zone presented earlier, focusing on one's position, calculating and predicting outcomes is typically the most prominent focus in this zone, which is a less optimal performance state. Therefore, positive reactions to errors in the Green Zone have much more to do with the overall attitude, focus and mindset the athlete demonstrates in this zone and far less to do with the score. When the athlete is focused on trying their best, the mindset is subconsciously pre-set to allow room for errors and they are simply playing the game, immersed in the moment, and going for it in their corresponding actions. This form of action is linked to a motivational style defined as 'approach motivation', where the athlete emphasises what they can do, rather than what they can't do or should avoid.

Young athletes have a natural predisposition to bounce back from errors when they are feel self-assured enough to play freely and try their best. This conclusion is based on the fact that the Green Zone information in Table 2 (summarising 150 young athletes' experience) was captured in the initial session, before they had begun formal mental-skills training. So, remarkably, there is an instinctual ability in young athletes to respond to mistakes and setbacks in resilient ways. I believe it is what we do as parents, teachers and coaches in our supporting role that can solidify or block this ability.

As competition experience grows, an emphasis on the absence of mistakes and a focus solely on results can set the athlete up to view their score or the absence of errors as their only indication of whether they are doing okay or not. The athlete uses the score to anchor their emotions, approach and mindset in a positive or negative way, making competitive experience like a roller coaster ride. An example of this in action is when an athlete's performance is dictated by the first few moments of their game or match. If they make a few errors or lose a few early points they may not recover, effectively losing confidence and spiralling downhill. Alternatively, if they play well in the first few moments of the game, they may essentially 'find their confidence' and build momentum nicely.

These dilemmas can become more difficult when the athlete's confidence is dependent solely on the score and the result. By understanding the ingredients in their Green Zone profile, they learn to build confidence on their *how*, their process, the things they can effectively control moment by moment. The elements in the Green Zone become their new ingredients for directing their competition experience and in time this leads to more consistent performances.

Triggers

Tables 4 and 5 introduce an important factor into the analysis of Red and Green Zones, which I refer to as 'triggers'. A trigger is an event, situation or perception that occurs directly before the competition, which can 'trigger' or initiate the characteristic thoughts and actions of either a Red or a Green Zone experience from the start of the match, race or round.

I have observed that specific expectations internalised by the young athlete before their match are the most dominant triggers in establishing Red and Green Zone experiences. The expectation of winning against an opponent perceived to be less skilled or less experienced is the most prevalent trigger for Red Zone experiences in young athletes.

The trigger can originate from a variety of sources, such as inoffensive and spontaneous talk about the opponent with friends or teammates at practice, previous encounters with the opponent, rankings and, most significantly, from messages and instructions given by parents before the competition, such as

'This is an easy opponent for you', or 'You should technically win this match if you just play your game.'

Messages that deliver a comparison to the opponent seem almost unavoidable for parents and coaches. With back-up from data, such as rankings or previous encounters with an opponent, these sorts of messages are not complete conjecture or exaggeration. If the facts support messages in your child's favour, why wouldn't you say it? I get it! At first glance, it's easy to assume that messages such as, 'This is an easy opponent for you', facilitate feelings of confidence and trigger Green Zone thoughts and actions in the match. However, with the help of the Red Zone chart in Table 4, we will break down how these messages can create expectations that have pervasive negative effects on your child's mindset and behaviours when competing.

Table 4: An example Red Zone demonstrating how a common trigger/ event influences the thoughts, feelings and actions experienced in junior tennis.

Triggers	Thoughts/ Focus	Feelings	Actions
	Questioning, doubting	Heightened negative reactions to mistakes	Desperate moves
Expecting to WIN. Against a player I 'should' beat	What am I doing? Are they better than me? What if I lose? I shouldn't be losing points I just want to get it over with. I don't want to be here	More nervous than usual More frustrated and angry than usual Shocked Embarrassed Feel like giving up	Hitting long often. Trying to close out points quickly Rushing routines Hands on hips between points, slumped Shouting at myself and my shots

Effort is de-emphasised as a focus on results is heightened

Heightened negative reactions to mistakes

Relaxed body + passive mind = complacent athlete

When athletes expect to win against a so-called 'weaker' opponent, they report feeling more relaxed before the match and during warm-up. However, they do not follow the thought process and action sequence that sets them up for peak performance. Typically, they don't think through their game plan or go over how they will apply their strengths or counter their opponent's weakness. Many athletes report low intensity in their warm-up, expressed as, 'going through the motions'. Their mind is switched off, more passive, and they are performing movements on autopilot, without much deliberate effort or focus. They might be thinking about what they are looking forward to doing after the match while going through their warm-up, for example. A relaxed body with a passive mind leads to a complacent athlete posed for an 'easy win'.

Without a solid warm-up the athlete is not activated or ready to compete. They can look like a slow starter, still warming up during the first game, first hole, or first quarter of the match. This makes the young athlete more vulnerable to unforced errors or atypical mistakes at the beginning of their performance. Unfortunately, it only takes one or two mistakes and a few lost points to shift from a state of relaxation to feeling progressively more tense or nervous, and it's not uncommon to see stronger emotional reactions and outbursts to errors than usual. In this case, mistakes are a threat to their self-image as the 'better' athlete and a threat to their 'easy win'. Therefore, it is no wonder their reactions to mistakes are more negative than usual.

The expectation that the young athlete 'should' win creates a results-only focus and lowers resilience from the set-up. Coupled with poor reactions to mistakes, the athlete does not respond well to their opponent's performance, is generally surprised when the opponent hits winners, and is more angered when the opponent gets a lucky break. In team sports, such as football, these negative reactions can be directed at their teammates' errors, or be projected toward referees. On top of this, the athlete who expects to win does not celebrate their well-played points or shots. Instead, they think, 'That's what I should be doing', and make it almost impossible to build positive momentum from solid execution.

In other words, they don't expect to be making silly errors, they don't expect a close match, and they certainty don't expect to be trailing their opponent at any point. What an athlete expects, or does not expect, to happen creates a set of rules to play by. The Red Zone chart shows how the expectation of winning can lead to a defeatist attitude and increases the likelihood of quitting behaviour, often in self-sabotage. That's because it's easier to protect your image if you lose without trying, and difficult to defend it if you go down fighting to the finish.

In Table 5, I provide insights into how the anticipation of a tough match, alongside the perception of the opponents being more skilled, can trigger a Green Zone experience. What you can see unfolding in the chart is an entirely different set of attitudes and behaviours to that displayed in Table 4's Red Zone. These attitudes all indicate high resilience and mental toughness.

From the athletes' accounts of their thoughts and focus, you can see how reduced expectations of winning contribute to an absence of thoughts about the result. Instead, a stronger emphasis on effort – such as to 'just try my best' – is revealed. The athlete is expecting a tough battle, which in some cases can lead to a spontaneous visualisation of themselves working hard, imagining long rallies, and chasing down the ball. Under these circumstances, it is more common for athletes to recount more clarity in their game plan. For example, 'I have a plan and I'll stick to it – to play to her weaknesses.' I have observed this also to be the case in team sports, such as football, where players and their coaches appear primed to discuss strategically how they will compete. In other words, you could say their 'head is in the game'. The Green Zone chart in Table 5 paints a clear picture of the antecedents of high-performance habits.

Table 5: An example Green Zone demonstrating how a common trigger/event influences the thoughts, feelings and actions experienced in junior tennis.

Expectation
and emphasis is
placed on effort

Triggers	Thoughts/ Focus	Feelings	Actions
Against a more experienced player. Not expected to win	Just try my best I have a plan and stick to it – to play to their weaknesses Focused on what my opponent is doing When I lose points, I tell myself 'it's OK' When I make a mistake, I shrug it off	Ready Focused Calm Not scared	Celebrating the points I win Using my forehand – my strengths Taking my time (at the back of the court, using my towel) My routine at serve is consistent Hitting hard Chasing every ball

Reactions to
mistakes are
positive and
productive

Pressure and
focus on attaining
a certain result is
reduced

Fighting spirit
and strong effort

You might expect a young athlete about to compete against an opponent perceived to be stronger to feel more nervous, anxious or scared. However, in their reflections, they consistently tell me it has the opposite emotional affect. While most report feeling more nervous before the match, their emotional experience during it is one of calmness, a feeling of being focused and the absence of fear. The corresponding actions are assertive, free from hesitation, and the athlete is more likely to celebrate good shots or points won, allowing momentum and confidence to build as the match progresses.

When preparing young athletes before a competition, it's common to prioritise building the athlete's confidence, boosting them up. It is natural to assume that it all comes down to confidence – the more they have, the less anxious or nervous the child should be, right? The Green Zone chart in Table 5 provides a different insight into mindset preparation for competition that reduces performance anxiety. At first glance sending your athlete the message 'You are not expected to win' might look antithetical to confidence building. When you look at the trigger in Table 5, these questions might automatically come to mind: 'If I send the message to my child that I don't expect them to win, isn't that going to knock their confidence?' or 'Isn't this like saying I don't think you can win, or I don't think you can do it?'

In order to answer these questions, you need to start by asking, 'What am I building my child's confidence to do?' Are you building their confidence to perform at their best, or to achieve a certain result? This very question is one of the most important checkpoints for your self-awareness as a facilitator of your child's growth as an athlete, and one that we will examine throughout this book. It is important to be aware of the difference between performance and results, because the child can control and directly influence only one of these factors – performance. Many parents talk about 'performance' when they actually mean 'results'. Performance is the input or the ingredients you mix together to maximise your chances of achieving the output – the result. Performance is not results. Results are results. Put another way, performance is the *how* and the results are the *what*.

In line with the focus of this chapter, the performance – the *how* – is the fusion of the key ingredients in the Green Zone (peak performance) or Red Zone (poor performance) charts.

The ingredients in the process taken from Table 2:

- thoughts and focus = 'focused on the ball/target'
- feelings = 'I feel relaxed and loose'
- actions = 'moving more, staying active, shaking out my arms, bouncing on my feet between points or plays'.

These specific ingredients in the form of thoughts, feelings and actions mix together to build the 'performance'. The results are simply the by-product of this Performance Process.

Building your child's confidence that they will out-perform their opponent is not true confidence at all; it is inflated hope. The result is something they do not have control over, and it is never a given that they will beat their opponent just because they are regarded as the stronger athlete (based on junior rankings or physical appearance). First, rankings are only useful for organising and structuring competitions. Beyond this, at the junior level, rankings are irrelevant and change like the wind. You should never use junior rankings to compare the skill, talent or ability of one young athlete to another. At this stage, every athlete is 'developing' these things, *and* at different rates. From my perspective, coping better with the competition environment than one's peers is reflected as a stronger ranking (another reason why I wrote this book).

Second, young athletes should never be expected to win just because they appear physically taller or stronger compared to their opponents of the same age. Genetics will only become truly advantageous much later in their development. This takes place when an athlete has mastered skills and techniques at a very high level in order to properly utilise their genetic gifts.

The message to your young athlete that they 'should' win the match becomes an expectation of results, and when that expectation exists the child, who does not have full control over it, naturally feels it as a source of pressure. What's worse, when your messages in preparation for a competition focus solely on predicted outcomes or expectations of the results, without any mention of the *how* on the performance side, the child's mind becomes fixed solely on the result – establishing a results-only focus.

This type of focus automatically leads to nervous self-talk such as, 'I hope I can do it', 'I hope I don't mess this up', or 'I hope I can win.' The key word in this internal dialogue is 'hope' – inflated hope, for that matter, which is the mind's subconscious recognition of not having full control over the expectation of winning. When hopeful thoughts are mixed together with doubts and worry, the athlete has the cognitive experience of anxiety.

Confidence

In the coming chapters we will explore various ways to build your athlete's true confidence before and after the game. From the information presented so far, it may seem that mentally preparing your athlete to face a challenging opponent and reducing expectations of winning are the best ways to build confidence before competing. Based on the evidence, there is no harm in this; you could start here and it can work nicely, but only in the short term. In the long run, these sorts of messages are not likely to foster consistent, deliberate execution of your athlete's Green Zone ingredients. Let me explain.

First, keep in mind that the information presented in these charts was recorded on my initial session with young athletes, before they had begun formal mental-skills training in their sport journey. This means that the thoughts, feelings and actions described in the charts are mostly instinctual, automatic thoughts and actions in reaction to the demands of the environment. Therefore, any messages that simulate the triggers from Table 5 can facilitate these instinctual high-performance habits, if the environment and the athlete's level of awareness remain roughly the same, which you already know is only possible in youth sport for a short period of time. The evolving nature of the demands of the competition include a lot of 'first time' experiences quite rapidly. Going from home court to local events, and then competing on the regional stage can influence thoughts and focus and the actions the athlete gravitates toward over time, not to mention the influence of changes in weather or pitch conditions. At first, the message 'I don't expect you to win', may reduce anxiety before a match. But over time, it won't help your athlete adapt or adjust to the ever-changing competition environment.

Second, the more competition experience your child gains, the harder it is for them to avoid making snap judgements about their opponent, and they will naturally form their own expectations of the results. Just one new competitive experience in a new environment, such as moving from home club friendlies to local events, can change the athlete's perceptions about their competition status and their competitors.

Lastly, let's look more closely at the quality or content of the message in effectively connecting the young athlete to their Performance Process or Green Zone ingredients. The message does reduce expectations on results, and generates a readiness to tackle a challenging competitor. However, it does not emphasise anything for the athlete to do or focus on. In other words, it doesn't stimulate the *how* to perform, which is the fundamental anchor for shaping consistently solid performances over time.

To build true confidence, your communication before and after the game has to emphasise and build expectations on the *how* or the Performance Process. In order to reach this point, you need to start by building awareness of your child's Green Zone ingredients. The strongest sense of awareness is built from the inside out. It is not something you can short-cut by telling your athlete what they should do with instructions and advice; the awareness of the Green Zone ingredients has to come from your child's perspective and experience. The best way to build this awareness is to start by asking questions after the game. Think about this activity like an appreciative inquiry, and approach it with curiosity. Go on a collaborative journey of exploration and discovery, because this is awareness building for you, just as much as it is for your athlete.

Building awareness with questions

When, where and how do you start? I understand that emotions can run high after the game. With this in mind we will go deeper into best, and worst, practices for debriefing and post-match discussions in the next chapter. To kickstart the exercise, opening with questions that capture the Green Zone experience is an inviting and positive approach. If your child has only just started competing, asking questions with curiosity and listening to their insights with interest will be well received, especially if you focus on their Green Zone experiences.

If your child has been competing for a while, and your typical debriefing process is met with great resistance or worse, you have been barred from debriefing practices altogether, I promise all is not lost.

The first step towards redemption is to sit down with your young athlete in neutral territory, away from their sport arena. Then explain the new approach to post-match discussions you want to try that can be more positive for both of you. The goal is to become more aware of the process together, which does not include the dissection of your child's mistakes. You should take the lead in terms of asking questions with curiosity, while your child leads the way in building insights and information. In addition, you may need to collaboratively reconsider where the best space or place is for the new post-match reflection. Directly after the game isn't typically the best time for athletes. Some athletes prefer to do this at the dining table before dinner, and if they have already developed a strong aversion to previous debriefing styles, it is okay to wait a day or two. The idea here is that agreeing to a time and space will establish commitment and increase the likelihood of getting that opportunity to set a new tone.

Key questions to build awareness

The flow chart below provides a variety of effective questions to build awareness of the Red and Green Zone profiles and smoothly transition from one category to the next.

Opening statements

- Green Zone: 'When the game was going well for you today...'
- Red Zone: 'When the game wasn't going well for you today...'

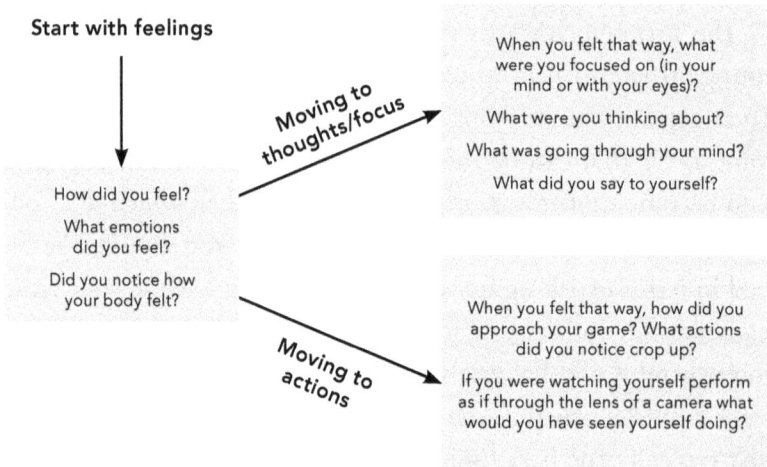

Start with feelings

How did you feel?

What emotions did you feel?

Did you notice how your body felt?

Moving to thoughts/focus

When you felt that way, what were you focused on (in your mind or with your eyes)?

What were you thinking about?

What was going through your mind?

What did you say to yourself?

Moving to actions

When you felt that way, how did you approach your game? What actions did you notice crop up?

If you were watching yourself perform as if through the lens of a camera what would you have seen yourself doing?

Supporting younger athletes

For parents and coaches of younger athletes, nine to 11 years of age, if you want to keep the post-game review light-hearted and less technical, you don't have to explicitly define Red Zone and Green Zone categories at first. Most younger athletes aren't aware of what a peak or sub-par performance actually is yet; they are more in tune with their feelings as an indicator of a good or a bad day. This is especially the case if your key message before matches is 'have fun', and your typical post-match question is 'Did you have fun today?' If this is the case for you, you can tap into their Green Zone by directly connecting it with the experience of fun or happiness.

Following are some ways to capture your child's experience and build the awareness of their process in simple ways.

Capturing the Green Zone

Opening Statement: When you were having fun and felt happiest in the game today...

- How did you approach your game?
- What did your movements and technique feel like?
- What did you do between points or plays when things were going well today?
- What were you thinking about or focused on?
- What were you saying to yourself?

Setting-up a contrast between the Green Zone and Red Zone can be the most effective way to draw out specific details from younger athletes.

Capturing the Red Zone

Opening Statement: When your felt annoyed, frustrated or down today…

- Did your actions change?
- What was different?
- What did your movements and technique feel like?
- Were there actions you stopped doing?
- What was your reaction to your errors or mistakes like?

Tips and tricks

- Start with questions that tap into Green Zone experiences first.
- Bring a curious mind and tone to this exercise.
- You don't have to ask all the questions I have suggested; one or two can be enough to bring the experience to life and avoid it feeling like an interrogation.
- With team sport athletes you can still ask all the questions from an individual viewpoint, because they always have their own role to play in the team.

Applying the information

Once you go through the exercise of building awareness of your athlete's Green Zone experience a few times, you will be less likely to offer vague pointers before their match, such as 'focus on the process today'. You now have specific details of your athlete's peak Performance Process and can encourage them to replicate one particular thought, focal point or action, prompting your child to focus more on the things that help them feel confident and in control. In this step, your child uses the Green Zone ingredients to develop an understanding of how to perform and the things they can control in their performance.

In becoming aware of their Red Zone ingredients, they can recognise much sooner in the match, race or round when they are off track and use their Green Zone ingredients strategically to shift out of the Red Zone quickly and proactively. Drawing from the Red Zone and Green Zone examples in Tables 1 and 2, the following is a visual representation of the active shift an athlete can initiate from Red to Green when competing.

An example of an athlete shifting from Red Zone to Green Zone in tennis or football/soccer.

The Red Zone

RECOGNISE – Watch out for these specific thoughts or actions

Thoughts & focus	Actions
'Don't mess this up' 'I can't do that again'	Hesitant and cautious with my movements Changing my technique often

↓

The Green Zone

REBOOT with this action and REFOCUS with this thought

Thoughts & focus	Actions
Focused on the ball or target	Chasing after the ball Staying active (shaking out body, bouncing on feet between points or plays)

In step one, the athlete has selected one specific thought and action in their Red Zone to watch out for or *recognise* in the match. In step two, the athlete has planned to engage one selected Green Zone action to *refresh* or *reboot* their game approach. The third and final step is to *refocus* using one selected Green Zone thought. On paper, it can seem like a slow sequence to work through, but in the game, the athlete will follow these steps in a matter of seconds.

Visualising this sequence before competing can help the child mentally rehearse these steps and connect with the thoughts and actions more strongly. What makes this system inviting and reassuring for even the youngest athletes to use, is the fact that the shift in focus and momentum is created with specific things the child already does naturally when they are performing well.

With the overall awareness of both performance states, the athlete learns that they don't have to stay in a Red Zone state waiting for the next race, match or the back nine holes in a golf round before they can hit the reset button or change gears. When they start poorly, or something isn't working, they do not have to hope for a great shot or play to magically appear. They can change and adapt rapidly, directly influencing this process from within.

I believe this realisation is one of the most important and empowering lessons for competition that a child can grasp.

QUICK POINTS

- The Red Zone represents low moments of competing, or the experience of sub-optimal performance.
- The Green Zone represents high points of competing, or the experience of peak performance.
- If you want to help your athlete to focus on the process, facilitating awareness of their Green Zone is the most important place to start.
- A strong awareness of the Green Zone protects against anxiety and fuels tenacity. Your athlete trusts that no matter what happens, even after a poor start or multiple errors, they can shift what's happening in simple ways they can control.
- Recognise–reboot–refocus.

CHAPTER 3

CONTROLLING THE MOTIVATIONAL CLIMATE

Athletes can develop in two distinct types of climates. One is like a pressure cooker, raising the heat and anxiety for the athlete in their sport. The other cultivates a cooler atmosphere for the athlete, where the potential for growth and positive energy is much higher.

What you say, think, and do over time will ultimately create one of these climates for your athlete. This chapter will help you see which climate you are creating, how it can impact your child's relationship with sport, and what to do to become a game changer in your athlete's journey.

Recognising performance anxiety

The formula for performance can be defined as:
performance = potential – interference.

One of the greatest factors to interfere with optimal performance and negate an athlete's true potential is performance anxiety.

Case 4: The case of the dedicated underperformer

Ian is a 15-year-old swimmer who is passionate and dedicated to his sport. He rarely misses a training session and he is known to be a hard worker in the pool. In our first session, Ian opens up about the immense frustration he usually feels following a meet (competition). He explains that he feels like a different swimmer in practice, his movements in the pool flow, his stroke feels effortless and his speed is there. But in competition, he feels heavy and his stroke is more robotic – less free-flowing.

What adds to the challenge is that most athletes who present a similar case to Ian's are aware of this issue for at least six months, sometimes for a year, before they seek help. By that time, the belief in their ability to compete has diminished, and the advice from their coach is often, 'You just need to work harder.'

Many parents and coaches don't realise that the most significant sign of performance anxiety is the discrepancy between training performance and competition. This is when the athlete's performance is significantly poorer in competition compared to simulated activities in training. Of course, you can expect such a discrepancy to occur if the athlete is inconsistent with training attendance or has been slacking in training and not putting in the effort required. But when you receive feedback from the coach that your child gives 110% effort in training all the time and they are dedicated to their sport, *consistent* poor performance in competition does not add up. Performance anxiety could very well be the principal factor in this case.

What do you see?	What do you hear?
Checklist of the signs and symptoms of performance anxiety • avoidance of training or competition • somatic complaints/aches and pains • disturbed sleep such as insomnia, or difficulty falling asleep or staying asleep • low appetite before competition • worry about other people's perceptions of their performance • focus on their peers and opponents in discussions (minimising their own potential and maximising others') • tiredness or fatigue • quieter than usual/ withdrawn • mood swings	Statements from an anxious athlete before competition • I am scared I'll perform badly • I'm scared to lose • I'm worried I will let my parents or my coach down

The difference between nervousness and anxiety

'I am not sure if my child is experiencing a strong feeling of nervousness, or if it is more like anxiety. What is the difference?' I often hear this valid question from parents in our initial conversation about their athlete's case. It lends itself to the importance of understanding the difference between nervousness and anxiety.

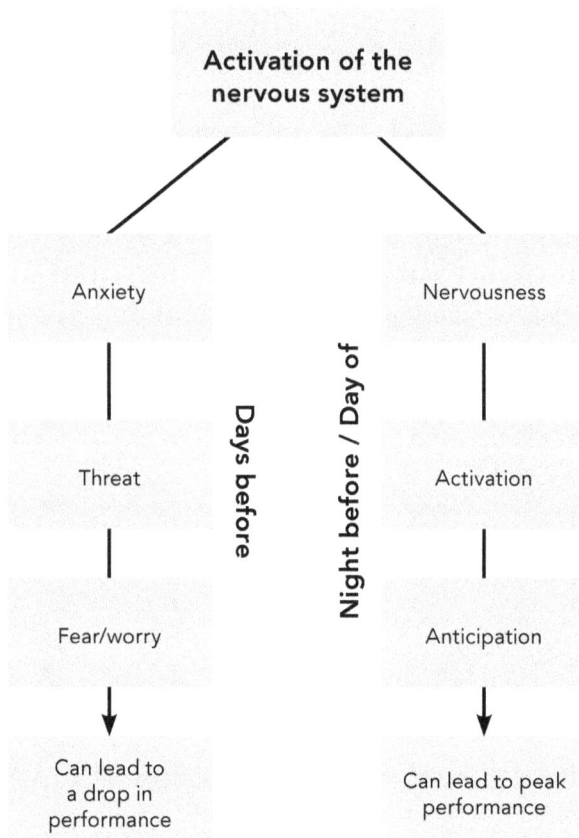

Activation of the nervous system

Anxiety	Days before	Night before / Day of	Nervousness
Threat			Activation
Fear/worry			Anticipation
Can lead to a drop in performance			Can lead to peak performance

If we only examine an athlete's physiological symptoms, nervousness and anxiety appear the same. The activation of the sympathetic nervous system, which we call the 'fight or flight' response, is most commonly experienced as sweaty palms, strong heartbeat, butterflies in the stomach, shaky limbs, muscle tension, dry mouth and multiple trips to the bathroom before their race. However, this is where the similarities between nervousness and anxiety end. What happens in the mind of an anxious athlete compared to a nervous athlete is a different experience.

Anxiety is experienced in the body *and* the mind. The mind of the anxious athlete is consumed with worry, fear and doubt expressed in the form of 'What if' statements focused primarily on negative possibilities; reminiscent of the Red Zone thoughts and focus presented in the previous chapter. The competitive arena is threatening and the athlete moves into red alert. In contrast, nervousness is experienced in the body without the worry, doubt and 'What ifs'.

Nervousness is the body's anticipation of a big moment or readiness for battle, and therefore sets in very close to the event (i.e., the night before or day of the competition). Anxiety, on the other hand, can develop many days, or even weeks before an event, contributing to sleepless nights, lower appetite and a much quieter or withdrawn child.

For some athletes, somatic complaints in the week leading up to an event can be an indication of performance anxiety. I have witnessed this most significantly in young gymnasts and dancers before major competitions. In these cases, sport specialised physiotherapists treating a young athlete in the week prior to their competition will observe their experience of niggling aches and pains, but be unable to detect any structural damage. In this instance, it does not necessarily mean that the young athlete is 'faking' these sensations (although this *can* occur in some cases to avoid competing). It can be explained by a hypersensitivity of the body, due to the heightened activation of the nervous system, or fight-or-flight response experienced with performance anxiety. Under these circumstances, the athlete has a strong need for control, which is associated with a hypervigilance of their body and excessive self-monitoring. Performance anxiety cannot lead to peak performance and 99% of the time it will contribute to suboptimal performance.

Nervousness, on the other hand, is useful and necessary for peak performance. The experience of nervousness is the body's chemical expression of adrenaline, which has been well documented in sport literature to facilitate performance. Adrenaline has been proven to enhance focus and increase tolerance to exertion pain. This means nervousness increases an athlete's ability to push their limits. In light of these findings, I prefer to relabel nervousness as 'activation' in mental skills training.

Most younger athletes (between 6 and 11 years old) perceive the onset of nervousness or activation to be a bad thing and associate the sensations in their body with poor performance. This is understandable when we view nervousness in the same way as the natural flight-or-fight response, telling us we are in a confronting situation. If you combine this instinctual reaction with common comments from parents such as, 'don't be nervous', or 'there's no need to be nervous', the child's negative perception of nervousness before big moments sticks pretty quickly.

It is not the degree of nervousness or activation that matters for great performances, so you shouldn't worry about your athlete feeling just the right amount, too little, or too much. What matters most in shaping positive coping is for your athlete to perceive the sensations of nervousness as positive, natural and helpful for performance.

To show you how young athletes can perceive nervousness in positive or negative ways, below are the results of an anonymous polling exercise in a mental skills training session with 24 boys and girls, aged between 12 and 15 years, competing in basketball, gymnastics, football and swimming. Each cloud reflects either positive or negative word associations for nervousness.

As you read these words, you can see the difference in the experience of nervousness when it is perceived as a negative or positive event when competing. You can see how valuable it is to help your athlete interpret the sensations of nervousness as useful for performance. It's the body letting the mind know it is ready to perform.

Brainstorm the negative feelings we connect or associate with nervousness

afraid **failure** useless
unconfident **failure** conflicted
self-doubt **worrying** uncomfortable
no-focus **helpless** scared
choking **helpless** hopeless
unprepared overwhelmed

Brainstorm the positive words connected to or associated with nervousness

passionate stong
energised **ready**
excited **prepared** motivated
normalcy **zone** **pumped** competitive
focused **anticipation**
adrenaline methodical

The intense heat of parental pressure

Young athletes' experience of anxiety in competition is primarily influenced by parents' actions and communication before, during and after the game. When you think about the negative impact parents can have on their child's relationship with sport, the words 'parental pressure' come to mind.

Parental pressure is a pattern of directive and controlling behaviour designed to trigger an athlete's responses and outcomes that are important to you as the parent. These actions could include communicating your expectations, unsolicited technical instructions and careful monitoring of your athlete's actions in practice and competition. Parents and coaches who are seen to be pressurising their athletes are typically described by others as pushy, controlling or interfering. These descriptions are consistent with the way this form of involvement is defined in research.

Parental pressure is generally assessed by asking the athlete questions such as:

- do your parents put pressure on you concerning your sport?
- how often or how much pressure do you feel your parents place on you?

These questions only consider the *frequency* or *intensity* of parental pressure, which means you can only conclude roughly whether or not there is too much pressure. When you only assess the intensity of behaviour, it is natural for parents to respond by asking:

- do I need to back off?
- is it best if I don't say anything and just leave him/her to it, or stop attending my child's matches for a while?

In this case, the one solution you have as a parent to ease anxiety is to reduce your involvement in some way. This boils down to reducing your presence, engagement and communication. You may remove the negative effect of pressure this way, but in doing so, you also seriously limit the support you could provide. So why is this the most common solution?

Time and time again, parents have expressed to me their utter disappointment with this type of advice given during parent seminars, or with restrictions imposed by their athlete's sports club about parental involvement. And to be fair, we must ask, isn't there a better way to prevent negative parental influence?

Reflecting on the relationship goals you set for your child in Chapter 1, if one of these goals was to achieve more quality time with your athlete, or create bonding opportunities, then it's only natural to find the recommendation to reduce involvement infuriating. There must be another way to approach this. And I believe there is. The question we need to answer is: how can I stay highly involved in my child's journey without creating pressure or anxiety?

To show you how it is possible to stay highly involved without creating pressure and anxiety, we have to look further than the *intensity* of pressure or parental involvement. We must also consider the *nature* of your involvement and in doing so, separate pressure from other types of involvement.

Intensity of involvement

Intensity is about your presence and level of engagement. How involved you are in supporting your child's league team, for instance, how often you attend training and competitions, and how frequently you direct your child's behaviour, offer advice, or give feedback.

Nature of involvement

The nature of your involvement creates a certain environment for your athlete, which psychologists refer to as a 'motivational atmosphere' or 'climate'. This climate directly influences your child's focus of attention in practice and competition; what motivates them to perform; and ultimately, how they define their success and failure. The climate is based on the expectations you emphasise, the focus of your feedback and conversations with your child about their sport and, most importantly, how *you* define their success.

The research in motivation science has found two distinct climate types:

- mastery-climate
- ego-climate.

A mastery-climate creates an environment in which effort, enjoyment and self-improvement are emphasised; mistakes are not punished but viewed as a medium for learning; and goals are set in the form of self-focused targets and striving for personal bests instead of being based on social comparisons.

In contrast, in an ego-climate, success is defined in terms of outperforming others with equal or less effort and mistakes are viewed as unacceptable.

GO TO Chapter 1 – Case 3: Teen athlete transitioning from sub-elite to elite ranks

If you look back at the third case example in Chapter 1, the tennis player Priya, I believe it shows the prototype of an athlete training and competing in an ego-climate. In this case example, when Priya is faced with the looming failure to win her match against a less experienced player, she abandons her process on the court, gives up and stops trying. For Priya, success is based on her ability to outperform others, so the game becomes more about managing others' impressions of her and preventing negative evaluations, rather than executing professional habits and giving maximum effort regardless of the score. Facing a challenge in a match reflects poorly on her status as a 'talented' athlete, and putting up a good fight with the potential threat of losing would compromise that reputation.

The research in youth sport to date has shown that parents, coaches and peers can impact an athlete's motivational climate independently, but parents' influence appears to be the most important of the three agents. The influence of parents and peers seem to be more significant than coaches for younger athletes between the ages of 9 and 15 years.

Athletes transitioning to elite ranks at around 15 years old spend an increasing amount of time with their coaches. This is when I believe the coaches' influence becomes more significant. Research has also found that adolescents trained by coaches who emphasise a mastery-focus experience less anxiety, higher self-esteem and greater enjoyment of their sport (McLaren, Eys & Murray, 2015; Smith, Smoll & Cumming, 2007). Boys and girls who report intentions to continue with their sport also report their coaches' actions and communication to promote a mastery-climate (Atkins, Johnson, Force & Petrie, 2015).

Peers influence each other's motivation through team behaviour. From interviews with boys and girls aged 12 to 16 years, Vazou and colleagues (2005) categorised the different ways that peers influenced athletes' perceptions of a mastery or an ego-climate. Team conflict during mini competitions and challenges at training, criticising each other's mistakes and the formation of cliques based on the evaluation of skill and ability were the primary actions that defined an ego-climate for these athletes. On the other hand, supporting each other to improve and being task-focused and emotionally supportive when players experienced disappointment were the actions that represented a mastery-climate for these athletes.

GO TO Chapter 1 – Case 2: The transition from 'just for fun' to 'more serious'

Look back at the second case example in Chapter 1, the football player Alvin. I believe it shows the stereotype of an athlete with a coach- and peer-induced ego-focus. Alvin has stopped enjoying his sport, he is anxious and dreads competing. A young athlete full of potential doesn't become unconfident and anxious purely because of some personality trait or vulnerability. Everything points to the motivational climate, which is in your hands as the child's parent, teacher or coach. Punishing mistakes by sending a player off the field and allowing verbal criticism to be the normal reaction in the team (because you think it reinforces high standards on the pitch) is completely off the mark. You are only breeding the dark side of perfectionism in your athletes that leads to tentative actions in competition (Appleton, Hall & Hill, 2011).

A young football player who is slow to react with the ball is second-guessing and indecisive because they are thinking about the mistakes they could make, rather than creating the play. The solution is not to instruct your athlete to work on their reaction time, the fix starts with you and their coach.

As parents, do not blindly follow these ideas without question. The dominant practices enforced in youth and elite sport are *not* the only way to train. It is easy to fall into the trap of an ego-focus in sport. My goal in sharing these insights is to prevent that from happening.

Table 6: A summary of the expectations that are emphasised, the atmosphere and the typical actions by coaches, parents and peers within an ego-climate.

	Ego-Climate	Influence and Atmosphere
Parent/ Coach	Outperforming others is emphasised	Anxiety
	Winning with less effort than others is reinforced	Pressure
	Results-focused competition is emphasised	Quitting
Coach	Mistakes are punishable (taken out of the game or told to run laps)	Perfectionist thoughts
		Higher risk of drop out
	Preferential treatment is given to certain players	Burnout
		Cheating
Peers	Competition amongst players is normalised, leading to team conflict and exclusion of players	Poor emotional control
	Judging and criticising peers' mistakes is normalised	

Table 7: A summary of the expectations that are emphasised, the atmosphere and the typical actions by coaches, parents and peers within a mastery-climate.

	Mastery-Climate	Influence and Atmosphere
Parent/Coach	Self-improvement and personal bests is emphasised	Persistence and fighting spirit
	Giving maximum effort regardless of score/results is reinforced	Positive response to challenge
	Task-focused competition is emphasised	
Coach	Mistakes are contingent; focus is on encouragement, instruction and learning	Greater enjoyment
	Roles are clear in teams and equality is the focus	Confidence / More likely to stay in sport
Peers	Coordinated team effort is normalised with a focus on helping each other improve	Cooperation / Friendship
	Emotional support is offered	Good sportsmanship

Comments from parents with a mastery vs ego focus

Gymnast's perspective

The gymnast returns home from training frustrated that she can't get the new skill that was introduced to her group today on floor. She kept trying repeatedly in training, but she couldn't execute the coach's corrections.

- **Ego-focus:** How did the other girls go with the new skill? Were they able to get it?
- **Mastery-focus:** How would you rate your effort today? The most important thing is that you tried your best and didn't give up, tomorrow is another chance to improve on it.

Tennis player's perspective

The tennis player finishes feeling happy with the result of her match, winning against a less skilled player.

- **Ego-focus:** Well done on the win, but the match was too close against that opponent, you are a much better player than her, I think you should have won by a bigger margin.
- **Mastery-focus:** Well done on the win today. What did you get out of today's match? Did you try something new you've been working on in training?

Swimmer's perspective

The swimmer comes over to the bleachers to greet his parents after getting a personal best in his main event and feeling happy with his swim.

- **Ego-focus:** You let your arch-rival beat you today. Did you see his time? No comment is made about the PB.
- **Mastery-focus:** Well done on getting a new personal best, how did you achieve that today?

What we see in a young athlete raised in a mastery-climate

What we see in gymnasts

The gymnast who is willing (nervous maybe, but not anxious) to integrate a new skill or transition into their routine for competition, even though the skill or move is not perfectly ready.

The mastery-climate influence

Being outside one's comfort zone is perceived as a sign of progress and success, not a lack of competency or ability. The athlete is less concerned about making errors because they are focused on putting forth effort to improve skills and see competition as an opportunity for learning, not achieving perfection.

What we see in tennis players

The tennis player that starts the match a long way behind in the first set (6-2) but responds with a fighting spirit, raising their game and intensity, in the final set losing in a tie-break.

The mastery-climate influence

Athletes with a mastery-focus will invest themselves in competitions even when they are not winning. In this case, the parents and coach have consistently communicated that trying your best is the most important thing and the athlete has internalised feelings of pride and success when giving maximum effort, regardless of the score or result.

What we see in swimmers

The swimmer that can follow their race plan instead of following the pack.

The mastery-climate influence

The athlete does not feel pressured to follow what their opponents are doing because they know their parents and coach are looking for self-improvement first and foremost and this requires them to focus on their own plan and technique in the pool.

What we see in team sports

The football player that feels accepted by his teammates and a strong sense of belonging on the team, and believes everyone has a distinct role to play in matches.

The mastery-climate influence

There is a unified team atmosphere in sports teams coached within a mastery-climate. Research by Ommundsen and colleagues (2005) studied 1719 young male and female

Norwegian soccer players, aged 12–19 years. Their findings revealed that both boys and girls reported stronger companionship and feelings of loyalty within their team when they perceived their coach to create a strong mastery-climate. This was achieved through clear role distinction between players, an emphasis on coordinated team effort, and focus on personal improvement.

What we see in a young athlete raised in an ego-climate

What we see in tennis players

The tennis player who struggles to perform at their usual standard or loses often against less experienced players, but to their parents' surprise, performs better than expected against older or more experienced opponents.

The ego-climate influence

The athlete views their success based on their ability to outperform others. The drive to protect their self-image and self-worth is strong when competing against a less experienced player, intensifying feelings of anxiety and pressure that diminish performance. Against a more experienced player, the athlete feels like they have nothing to lose; negative evaluations about their skill, ability or ranking are less likely even if they lose, anxiety is low, and concern about mistakes is lower too, freeing the athlete up to play at their best.

What we see in swimmers

The swimmer that is consistently injured or has the flu the week before every meet.

The ego-climate influence

Athletes who embrace their sport journey know that training is the focal point of that journey, while competitions mark the celebration of that journey to date. Young athletes raised in an ego-climate do not view training in this way. They see training as a means to an end – it's what you have to do to prepare for the next meet. Their focus and striving are short-term and cyclical – from one meet to the next, like a rat running on the wheel. When one meet is done, they start over again. These athletes are prone to cramming before meets, meaning that they ramp up their effort in training dramatically as the meet approaches. Add a dose of pre-comp anxiety in there and you have an athlete prone to getting sick before every meet.

This type of relationship with sport is built from the great importance placed on results, alongside a poor understanding of the sport journey and lack of emphasis placed on the process. Doing well in races is very important to these athletes, but they do not deliberately focus on improving race elements in training, such as mastering technique, improving their kick, body position, turns. All these things are out of sight, out of mind. Instead they think only about the target time. It doesn't matter if it's club night or national champs, every meet is crucially important to hit a new personal best.

Another example in swimmers

The swimmer who is most satisfied with their training when they can hit the target times while putting in less effort than their teammates.

The ego-climate influence
What matters most is getting the desired result, and if you can achieve it with less effort than others, even better! Effort is not part of their model of success. Young athletes with an ego-focus tend to believe that an athlete who is putting in more effort than their peers to get the desired result is less skilled and less talented.

What we see in golfers
The golfer who hits three consecutive balls off the tee out of bounds with no adjustments and no pre-shot routine, picking up their ball on the 16th hole to disqualify themselves to avoid posting a score and blaming the course for their game.

The ego-climate influence
When winning or finishing with respectable performance seems out of reach, self-sabotage is common in athletes with an ego-focus, because self-preservation is so important in the face of failure and performing worse than one's peers is unbearable. It is not uncommon for young athletes with a strong ego-motivation to resort to cheating and demonstrating poor sportsmanship because they are prone to feeling unhealthy negative emotions such as desperation in the competition setting. Such behaviour is not at all excusable. The point I am making here is that it is important to understand the motivation behind young athletes' patterns of behaviour, because there is a stronger root cause that you might not realise. The climate you create for your athletes really has the power to define the relationship they have with sport, their teammates and their competitors. I firmly believe that teaching young athletes good sportsmanship starts with creating the right

motivational climate and an ego-climate does not facilitate good sportsmanship.

Mixing pressure with motivation

O'Rourke and colleagues (2011) set out to understand how motivational climate and pressure initiated by parents might influence athletes' experience of anxiety. They studied 307 boys and girls who had been swimming competitively since age seven, aged between 9 and 14 years old at the time of the study. Swimmers rated their level of anxiety at the start, middle and end of the season. Each swimmer completed questionnaires that examined how often they experienced parental pressure before, during and after competitions, with questions such as 'Do your parents get upset with you if they think your swimming is not going as well as it should be?' Swimmers also rated how strongly they agreed or disagreed with statements that assessed their perception of a parent mastery-climate such as, 'I feel my mother/father/guardian is most satisfied when I learn something new', and statements that examined the presence of a parent ego-climate such as, 'I feel my parents look most satisfied when I win without effort.'

Across the season, the highest levels of anxiety occurred in swimmers who reported high parental pressure and a strong ego-climate. This means that when parents are more forceful and explicit in conveying their expectations based on out-performing others, and deem errors unacceptable, evaluative pressure is high and the child's degree of control over the desired result is low. This raises anxiety considerably. Based on our journey in this chapter so far, you probably aren't surprised by this finding.

What was surprising in the study, though, was the finding that at all time points in the season, the swimmers with the lowest levels of anxiety reported *high* parental pressure within the context of a strong mastery-climate. This means mastery-climate is remarkably protective. Parents who engage more intensely and persistently with their child to focus on self-improvement and encourage effort and learning from mistakes reduce evaluative pressures. They emphasise those factors over which the child has greater control. This minimises anxiety in the competition arena.

These results suggest that the influence of the motivational climate you create for your child is amplified when you are highly involved. As a parent you can be highly involved in your child's sport journey but the stronger your involvement becomes, the more crucial it is to pay extra close attention to the motivational climate you are creating.

If you are highly involved but convey an ego-climate, the consequences for your child's development in sport can be detrimental. However, the more you create a mastery-climate in your involvement, the more your athlete will thrive and your relationship through sport will strengthen. I find this the most valuable piece of insight I can share to give you peace of mind: what you do, think, and say will always carry positive weight when you work hard to build a mastery-climate focus in yourself and your child.

A cautionary note on pressure

This is not to say that parental pressure is good. It doesn't matter if you are aware of your actions or not, when you apply pressure, you will come across as highly directive or demanding, and you will be exerting control over the athlete. When you do this, the athlete's sense of control over their participation or performance drops and anxiety always increases. For example, messages such as 'you have to perform well in this competition', or 'I expect you to beat your opponent', both apply pressure because they are demanding in tone and focus only on the results, which you know now the athlete has a low degree of control over.

O'Rourke's study (O'Rourke et al., 2011), found that anxiety was minimal and generally stable across the season for swimmers who reported low levels of parental pressure regardless of the motivational climate their parents created. Low levels of parent engagement mean a 'no harm done' situation, even if the parent has an ego-oriented conception of success. But with less parental influence and involvement, the athlete is more susceptible to the motivational climate initiated by coaches and peers.

Motivation without pressure

I believe that an ego-climate and parental pressure go hand in hand. When you create a strong ego-climate for your child in their sport journey, they will feel evaluative pressure, and feel the need to beat other children to affirm their progress and talent and to win your approval. Success is measured solely by their ability to outperform others, and when they lose more often than they win (which is normal in sport), their belief in their ability suffers. On top of that, they are driven toward goals over which they have limited control. So, after a while, they can feel like they are fighting a losing battle. It's luck or by chance that things will come together, or the hope that their opponent messes up.

When the feeling of control over one's performance is low, the inner drive will not be there. Parents try to compensate with overtly directive behaviour, and appear to be using more energy on the sidelines than their athlete does in the match. Attempts to motivate your athlete can become overbearing and pressurising very quickly. Over time, you will be the hardest working parents in the club, with the athlete that puts in the least amount of effort.

'If I don't try, I won't care and when I lose, it doesn't hurt as much.' This is what I hear from young athletes who have learnt to use less effort as a protective coping strategy in competition.

The bottom line is, you cannot shape a confident and gritty athlete in an ego-climate. If you want your child to develop that inner drive and motivation, you must work harder to create the mastery-climate.

Start by asking good questions with genuine curiosity to trigger self-awareness and shape an independent mind when your athlete trains and competes. You do not need to be as directive or instructive as you think, or play the advisor or performance analyst. You need to be the facilitator and awareness builder. Don't be the director, be the collaborator or partner–mentor in their sport journey.

The best place to start is by asking the questions outlined in Chapter 2 to facilitate the awareness of their Red and Green Zones. I cannot emphasise enough how valuable these questions can be, even when done in informal ways. This is the perfect exercise for building a mastery-climate and igniting your athletes' interest in mastering the process. The more these learnings and insights can come from them, the more confident they will be to direct their performance, and it's your job to facilitate that. Always keep in mind that when an athlete knows how to take control of themselves and their performance the inner drive will be there.

Pressure and punishment

Laziness is not a reasonable explanation for behaviour. Every action is motivated by something, even the lack of action. All children innately want to please their parents and perform well in competition. So why would an athlete look like they don't care, refuse to follow their game plan, or tank matches (give up) even when they are the most talented? By now, you will recognise that these behaviours are a by-product of an ego-focus, which is established first and foremost by the ego-climate you shape.

Punishing your child for tanking or not following their plan will create pressure and intensify their ego-focus. Your child's attitude and behaviour reflect the climate you create; it starts with you. The worst type of punishment I see is when parents or coaches bar their athletes from going to training when they perform poorly, or prescribe fitness activities as a form of punishment. These activities are the heart and soul of a mastery-climate. You cannot have a task-focus if you do not foster a love for fitness and training. You can make your athlete aware of behaviours that are undesirable with debrief conversations about their Red Zone, but punishment is always counterproductive. If your athlete has been labeled talented or you know they are a high achiever, then they already beat themselves up enough for losing or performing poorly. Your job is to help them build awareness of their Green Zone, value professional habits in their process and create the mastery-focus that leads to positive actions in the competitive arena.

Supporting the drive from within

You have to be an advocate for high standards in the process, and you have to help your child value all the habits before, during and after the game, just as much as they do the results.

GO TO Chapter 1 – Process vs results

In Chapter 1, you outlined a series of habits and actions that you value most in your child's sport. Start conversations about these habits with your athlete and collaboratively discuss how to make these habits stronger in training first and eventually apply them to competition.

Creating conversations that spark interest in, and show the importance of building high standards in the process shapes the mastery-focus. This is because it creates a positive drive and pushes toward improving habits and skill-mastery over which your child can take ownership. You do not need to have all the answers or know your child's sport deeply to engage in these conversations. You will be surprised by how much your athlete knows and what they will bring to the table. This is why I recommend you make all your post-match debrief sessions and discussions collaborative; start with questions not instructions.

Applying the information

GO TO Chapter 1 – Parent goals

Setting mastery-focused goals

Review the goals you set in chapter 1. Can you adjust any of these to include more goals that are mastery-focused and less that are ego-focused? Keep in mind, goals that are focused on improving skills and trying new things are more mastery-focused, while goals that are about seeing your child compare well to other athletes are ego-focused.

Refining goals

Ask your child which skills they would like to learn or improve this season, or if there is something new they can try this season? Don't worry if you feel your knowledge of your child's sport is lacking, ask for their input.

Tip for commitment

Bring these goals to life for your child by asking them to write them down. This action creates stronger commitment.

Identity goals

If you did specify goals such as projecting a good image or reputation, it is important to reduce concerns about other parents' perceptions or winning other's approval. Make sure these identity goals come from, and can be assessed by, the athlete on their own. You can do this by asking yourself and your child 'Which personal qualities (e.g., work ethic) and skills (e.g., agility) do you feel are important for being the best athlete you can be?' This will help your athlete take ownership of building their self-identity in their sport. You may want to refer to the table you created in Chapter 1. This exercise was the starting point for looking into the habits for growth and development that you and your child value the most.

Relationship goals

These goals, which focus on showing good sportsmanship, teamwork and encouraging others, are all effective ways to enhance the mastery-focus in your child's sport.

Green Zone goals

Once your child builds awareness of their Green Zone actions, they can set focus-goals to activate these habits in competition. For example:

- **Green Zone action:** positive body language – head up, eyes up, bounce on toes
- **focus-goal:** between points and when I make mistakes – I'll focus on my positive body language.

You *can* set goals around the results

Yes, of course you can set results-focused goals such as winning, score, medal, ranking. Shoot for the stars! Just remember these points:

- adjust your language – result goals cannot be expectations, they are goals to strive for, to chase, to aim for, but they are not a given
- once the result goal is set (the *what*), bring the focus back to the *how* – the mastery goals or Green Zone actions for the competition
- de-emphasise results – after the game, assess or discuss effort, intensity and focus *before* talking about the results.

If you have a competitive child

You do not have to stop your child competing against their peers in the hopes of reducing an ego-climate. You just have to be mindful that this doesn't define how you or your child view their overall ability, or success or failure in their sport. I recommend that athletes play to their strengths, and if your child loves to compete, by all means encourage those duels with their buddies and your child's desire to be the best. Just keep in mind the following points.

- Remember that if the child wins, it does not mean they are a better athlete, and if they lose it does not mean they have less ability.
- Remember that winning or losing is an isolated moment on a given day and event, it does not define their success or failure.
- Always refer to your athlete's self-referenced goals.
- Always ask about their effort first *before* who won or lost.
- Take opportunities to reference other athletes who are elite or professional that your child looks up to. They can research these elite athletes' milestones and personal bests as results to strive for. The emphasis should be on understanding the habits and character of their idols, reinforcing the process and development of professional habits as important for growing into an elite athlete.

Looking ahead

In Chapter 4, we will look specifically at how to optimise your support before, during and after the game. If you are still unsure about what to do, think or say in these key moments, don't worry. The next chapter will provide guidance and tools to help you connect the dots from the previous chapters.

QUICK POINTS

- An ego-climate and parental pressure go hand in hand. You cannot shape a confident and gritty athlete in an ego-climate. If you want your child to develop inner drive and motivation, you must create a mastery-climate.
- Shaping your athlete's inner drive won't happen by instructing or directing your child. Be their collaborator. Ask curious questions that help to encourage and increase their passion in mastering the process.
- If you and your child want to narrow your focus to a few habits in their Performance Process, make it these three:
  - effort
  - determined self-talk
  - positive reactions to mistakes.

CHAPTER 4

THE POWER OF EMPATHY AND ATTENTIVE SILENCE

At some point in this book, you might have wondered what my sport journey was like with my parents. Both my dad and mum were invested in my golf career, but my relationship with my dad in the journey is more significant. The bond I shared with my dad, Michael, through playing competitive golf defined our relationship when I was young, and it still does to this day.

Case 5: Me and my dad

I'd say my dad is the quintessential Australian guy. He's hard working, laid-back and he loves his sport. Growing up, the weekends in our house were all about sport. If we weren't playing it, we would be watching it. First the cricket, then probably tennis followed by golf, and Sundays were for watching football. My dad started my sisters and me playing golf when we were young; I was six years old. I have a twin sister, Carly, and a younger sister, Elodie, and all three of us were accomplished players in our own right. When my twin and I were 12, my parents relocated us from the suburbs to live on the 15th hole of a championship golf course to support our ambitions. My dad spent every weekend and all the school holidays driving us around the state to compete in tournaments. He drove more than one hour each way to work and back, but no matter what, if I asked for his help when he came home at the end of the day, he would always help me practice until after dark. He was very busy, but I never remember him saying he had other things to attend to.

I want to share with you two defining moments with my dad in my sport journey. These moments are not about celebrating a big win or milestone. They are significant because of the way Dad supported me, which had a profound impact on my journey, my relationship with him, and with sport.

The young athletes and the parents I have worked with over the years are my biggest inspirations for this book, but my sport journey with my dad is too. I am deeply passionate about supporting the parent–athlete relationship because I know what a strong impact it can have on an athlete's life.

My first national golf championship

When I was 14, I was one of six girls under the age of 18 selected to represent the state of Western Australia at the Australian Junior Interstate Series. At that age, this is the event to aim for. It means you have made it to the top junior ranks in your state and it's an exciting chance to face off against six other state teams in the country. I played in the interstate series for five consecutive years, but the first was the most memorable, because it was played in my home city of Perth. My dad was there to watch me play some of the best golf I'd ever played up until that point in my junior career.

It was my first time in a major competition and I felt exceptionally confident in my game. I was playing on auto-pilot, with no thought at all over the ball. I remember the feeling well, because it was the first time that I was really aware of my mind being clear of thought. I had complete trust in my swing and body. It was the peak of summer in Australia and the tournament demanded 36 holes of play each day, for multiple days in a row. In golf, this is like a marathon. On one particular afternoon, it was 36°C, but I didn't feel a thing, I was immersed in the game. We were playing against the New South Wales team, who were dominant in the series.

My dad had taken a few hours off from work in the afternoon to stop by and watch me play the match; I still remember what he was wearing. A long-sleeve, light-blue dress shirt and pants, tie and all, he must have been roasting in his uniform, but true to his form, you'd never know, because my dad wouldn't mention it. He walked slowly and quietly about 50 metres behind me in the rough off the fairway. He probably wanted to make sure I wasn't feeling nervous or distracted with him there, he walked so far behind me. Every single shot I played felt great, and I remember looking for him on just about every shot and putt I hit. He would do this reassuring nod of his head, as if to say, 'Good shot, keep it up, stay focused.' If I hit an exceptional shot, I'd turn back to face him after I hit the ball and he nodded with a smile and clapped his hands so subtly it didn't make a sound. My dad would do that same action every time. I still remember to this day how that quiet gesture filled me up with such encouragement, and how it propelled me forward, like a strong reminder to 'keep it up', 'stay patient' and 'play one shot at a time'.

My dad didn't get to watch me finish, but I called him straight after the round to tell him I won my match. No matter the event, and all the way through to my college golf days, when I shared the news of a great round, my dad responded with the same feeling in his voice, the sort of reaction you can anticipate over time and look forward to hearing. A composed mix of delight and pride with his words, 'That's fantastic news, darl, I'm really proud of you.' I would describe every detail of my great shots – the yardage, the wind direction, where the pin was, and how I saw the shot – the full picture. There is nothing better than recapping every detail of your great shots with your dad until it's etched in your mind.

What the research says about my dad's actions

I have often wondered why my dad's subtle actions of encouragement stand out so strongly, even to this day. What insights can the research give us? Interestingly, one study exploring child preferences for parent involvement in youth sport has found that young athletes between 7 and 14 years old have a strong preference for *attentive silence* (Omli & Wiese-Bjornstal, 2011). This involves sitting down quietly, controlling your emotions and maintaining a positive attitude while 'paying attention' to the match. Children indicated that parents should 'sit down quietly and that's about it' (10-year-old girl) or 'sit down quietly and not yell out comments' (10-year-old boy).

Parents, coaches and teachers are too often concerned about finding the right words, or not saying the wrong things to their athletes. But subtle gestures of encouragement or understanding can have more impact than words. Attentive silence allows parents to be supportive without the risk of becoming a source of distraction or embarrassment for young athletes. Similar preferences were indicated for giving praise. Young athletes prefer to receive praise when they come off the field to the sidelines, because when they are out in the action, it can be distracting. These findings echo what I hear from young athletes in my sessions. When we discuss their preferences for parental support from the sidelines, young athletes often tell me that they want attentiveness and gestures of encouragement, but comments during the game, even if they are encouraging, can be distracting. It is hard for the child to focus on the game and also focus on what you, their parent, are saying.

A tough lesson with my dad by my side

According to the Kids Speak study (Omli & Wiese-Bjornstal, 2011), encouragement as a response to mistakes and empathy toward your athlete, their opponents and even the referees is important to young athletes. This was certainly true for me growing up. I have so many memories of my dad being by my side when I won, when I lost, or when I experienced one of those heart-breaking moments that become the best lessons along the way.

One of the most memorable of these difficult moments was in a competition in the Chicago area the year before I started college. My parents had moved to the US for my dad's work commitments and I was visiting them during the summer. I played in a regional tournament and Dad caddied for me. The decision to play was made on short notice. So, I hadn't seen the course before I played it and after a pretty average front nine, I knuckled down on the second nine and played lights out.

On the final hole of the day, I had a very short one-foot putt for a two-way tie for first place. I walked up to the putt, making an awkward stance to avoid my playing partner's line to the hole, and without any preparation I hit the putt and missed the hole completely, to lose the tournament by one shot. It was one of those moments that passes by in the blink of an eye. In less than five seconds you go from feeling on top of the world to overwhelming regret, wishing you could take back that one stupid careless action and replay the shot again.

I didn't care about the loss as much as the shockingly careless mistake. I was so upset that I kept saying over and over, 'Why did I do that, how could I be so stupid?' I will never forget how my dad responded to this.

He nodded, gave me a hug and said, 'These things happen, I really feel for you, darl. You played a great round and, you know what, you'll probably never make that mistake again.'

He could have said so many things out of his own frustration and desire for me to win, but what I remember is his empathy. That is one thing I always felt strongly when I had setbacks and disappointments. Right after the game, Dad never used the moment to go back over the mistakes or make a point of saying, 'You should've done this...', or 'Why didn't you play it that way?' He was empathetic and encouraging in those moments and that's all.

By the time we drove out of the parking lot that day to head home, I had let it go, trying hard to focus on the lesson. I know deep down that I would not have felt that way or been able to move on so quickly if my dad hadn't reacted the way he did.

The tough talks

It wasn't *always* rosy in my sport journey with my dad. We also had difficult debriefs following competitions from time to time. When I played poorly or was going through a performance slump we had frustrating discussions, trying to hash out why I didn't play well and what had gone wrong. I remember what I felt during these debriefs – extreme disappointment and frustration. I do not remember any of the important lessons, advice or instructions my dad imparted. Sorry, Dad! I suppose I mentally blocked it out and eventually moved on, once the emotions subsided.

According to the research on this, it is common for young athletes to attempt to mentally block out comments when conversations after the game are upsetting. Pretending to be asleep on the car ride home, giving parents the silent treatment and listening to music are common strategies young athletes use to avoid difficult conversations post-competition (Tamminen, Poucher & Povilaitis, 2017).

The study by Tamminen and colleagues, exploring how young athletes 11–16 years of age deal with upsetting conversations in the car ride home, reported such comments as: 'When my dad's mean to me after the game, I don't even take it personally anymore. I get that I played bad but I'm not going to let him bug me about it.' And 'I don't like it on the car ride home when he's talking about me playing badly. And I'm thinking, Okay, get home, get in the shower and you can have your thirty minutes of peace.'

Although parents believe that difficult conversations following poor performances create teachable moments, I do not agree. It seems that young athletes are more inclined to 'wait it out' instead of taking in the advice, or they mentally block out the conversation. This was true for me in my experience as a young athlete some time ago, and it's still true for athletes in this generation. There has to be a better way to negotiate difficult moments following poor performances and capture the teachable moments in the car ride home. In the following chapters, I will share the best ways to support your child before, during and after the game, introducing novel tools for debriefing sessions and strategies for the car ride home.

QUICK POINTS

- You do not need to do or say as much as you think.
- Practicing attentive silence can be one of the most effective ways to show your support from the sidelines.

CHAPTER 5
BEFORE THE GAME

One week to go		Night before		Game day

▲

Case 6: Seeking perfect preparation

Arena is a 15-year-old badminton player who experiences performance anxiety before competing. She likes to make sure she does all the right things in the lead-up to events. Her parents are supportive of her preparation and remind her to go to bed early and eat well in the lead-up to the competition.

Arena explains, 'The week before a big competition I start to feel pretty tense and the things my parents say make me feel more stressed. I know my mum is trying to help, but I feel more stressed when she reminds me to eat this so I have more energy, and to go to bed early, and not to forget things and drink more water.'

During the week before a competition, Arena frequently monitors how she feels, tuning into even the slightest aches or pains and signs of fatigue. These signs only increase the anxiety she feels; she worries that she is not doing the right things, and goes over the 'What ifs' about not performing well.

Take the pressure off

I often hear these comments from athletes between the ages of 12 and 15. It might seem helpful to remind your child to elevate their habits the week before a major competition, but it can actually add to their feelings of tension and stress that can build as the competition gets closer. When we try to elevate habits the week before, the focus of the week becomes about perfecting preparation. This mindset can lead athletes to assume perfect preparation is needed in order to perform at their best, and this is not realistic or necessary. For instance, when an athlete feels more tired than usual, they skip breakfast, or they didn't sleep well the night before the race, they can assume they are less likely to perform well. When young athletes focus on perfecting their preparation the week before a competition, they place more limitations on themselves when things aren't *perfect*, and this can become exaggerated over time.

Most athletes do not figure out the right preparation routine for themselves until their late teens or even later in their career. If you feel your child's habits could be better to facilitate performance, the week before the meet is *not* the time to start making big changes. Habits that support peak performance should be enforced as part of their daily routine weeks or even months before major competitions. Your child is better off sticking to their usual routine than making major changes a few days before the event.

The key message you want to send to your athlete is: there is no such thing as perfect preparation. At the elite level, athletes and their coaches strive to execute the ideal plan and hope for best-case scenarios, but rarely does anything go according to the ideal plan. Small adjustments before and during the competition are the key to getting close to the ideal scenario. To reduce anxiety, worry and doubt the week before a competition, encourage your athlete to be flexible and adaptable.

The focus around preparing should be about compensating and adjusting, as much as possible. For example, if your athlete wakes up tired, remind them this is okay, emphasise that they can adjust how they feel, and focus on problem solving as part of good preparation. Talk about ways they can raise their energy by playing music, staying active and bouncing on their feet instead of sitting still. Remember 'motion changes emotion'.

Facing fears and worst-case scenarios

One week before competition is when an athlete's fears, doubts and worries about competing will surface, and they may bring them up to you in the form of 'Dad, what if...?' I understand that parents do not want to make a big deal out of things that could be irrational, or make the fear seem more real by talking about it. If this is your concern, then you are likely to try to tone down your athlete's worries by saying something like, 'don't worry, that's not going to happen,' and change the subject to more positive possibilities. This is okay for those highly irrational worries, however, not all your child's fears are totally irrational and unrealistic. As a matter of fact, most young athletes express concerns about worst-case scenarios that their peers or idols have experienced, such as a swimmer's goggles falling off in the middle of a race, a golfer's ball moving at address, or a tennis player's strings breaking mid-rally.

Although these unfortunate events are rare, they will likely happen more than once in a child's journey to becoming an elite athlete. So, it is a good idea to talk about the worst-case scenarios when your young athlete brings them to the table. First, remove the fear by reassuring your athlete that it is all right if these events actually happen. Say, 'These situations do not have to affect your performance, if you respond well and keep your mind on task', or 'You can't control when it happens, but you can control how you respond to these events.' Brainstorm with your athlete the positive ways in which they can react if these events arise. Come at it from a problem-solving angle and a logical approach.

Swimming legend Michael Phelps famously credits his success in the 200m butterfly at the Beijing Olympics in 2008 to his preparation for unfortunate events (Owaves, 2016). Phelps won gold and set a world record despite not being able to see for the last 75m, when water filled up his goggles. To prepare for this, he would visualise performing the exact number of strokes it took to swim the race, in case his goggles fell off and he couldn't see.

There is no such thing as the perfect plan, perfect race or perfect match. Being a great competitor is about knowing how to compensate and adjust as you go, to get as close as you can to your best performance.

Talking about results

The week before the competition is not a good time to emphasise the results your athlete is aiming to achieve. Goal setting and discussions about results should be done weeks before the competition, as a way to direct your athlete's motivation and focus in training. As the event comes closer, a results-only focus is not helpful. The athlete has a low degree of control over outcomes at this stage, so focusing on this directly before competition elevates anxiety and pressure. Instead of focusing on the *what* (the results), focus on the *how* (the process).

The week before the event is the time to set your athlete's sights on executing their Green Zone thoughts and actions in competition (see Chapter 2). Your athlete has a high degree of control over these habits and they know these habits lead to peak performance. Your child will feel more confident and excited about competing when you talk about these things with them.

GO TO Chapter 1 – Process vs results

Consider the chart in Chapter 1, about capturing the habits you value most in your child's sport. Ask your athlete the question, 'which one or two habits would you like to focus on the most in your upcoming competition?'

Example in swimming

The habits you value most in your child's sport	What it looks like in action
Starting strong and assertive in a race	Exploding off the blocks. In the race. Head down, not watching or following other lanes.
Bouncing back from mistakes or set-backs	Moving on quickly after a race – listening to music, eating, talking with friends in the stands, looking forward to the next race – showing positive body language around the pool.
Encouraging clubmates	A positive gesture or verbal comment directly after a clubmates' race, cheering a club mate on from the stands.

To give your athlete a sense of ownership over their performance, allow them to make the selections independently

Maintaining consistent routines	In the stands – putting on a tracksuit and staying warm, eating, listening to music; in the marshalling area – stretching, staying loose, smiling.
Displaying positive body language and presentation habits	At blocks – taking a deep ready breath, shaking out body or power pose; for some, a wave to the stands, smiling.
Being receptive to feedback and respecting the coach or other authoritative figures	Approaching the coach after a race; nodding to the coach's instructions, open body language and eye contact.

To give your athlete a sense of ownership over their performance, allow them to make the selections independently

Emphasise the 'how'

Ask your athlete, 'How will you bounce back from mistakes and show positive body language?', 'What would you like to do?' or 'When do you want to do [these actions]?'

Your athlete can mention the actions you have written in the chart or offer new ones. Once again, it is important to let them choose and give them ownership over the actions they want to perform.

Building true confidence

Through these steps, the goals and expectations of your athlete for the upcoming event aren't just focused on outcomes. The expectations are now focused on performing the key actions they have chosen with full commitment when the opportunity arises.

Remind your athlete that 'When you bring more focus to bouncing back from mistakes and positive body language in your next competition, it can give you the best opportunity to perform at your best.' With this message, you are not providing hope or vague encouragement such as, 'Don't worry, you can do it.' You are building *true* confidence. That is because this message is based on the facts about your athlete's Performance Process and it directs their focus to things they can control.

Talking to teens

Help your athlete connect with their Green Zone. Start by asking questions with curiosity that establish how your athlete wants to feel when they compete. This reminds your child they can control how they want to feel and that is always empowering.

Questions you can ask with example athlete responses:

Parent: How would you like to feel during your next competition?
Athlete: Happy, relaxed and confident.
Parent: To help you feel that way, what would you like to focus on or think about when competing?

Athlete: Focus on the ball, think one point at a time.

Parent: What would you like to do to help you feel this way? Think about your actions on the court.

Athlete: Chase more after the ball, play aggressive and encourage myself.

Tip: The level of awareness and understanding in your athlete's responses will depend on your commitment to debriefing about their Red Zone and Green Zone experiences in previous competitions (see Chapter 2). Collaborative reflection of their Green Zone experiences is particularly important for your athlete to feel confident going into the next event.

GO TO Chapter 2 – Key questions to build awareness

Green Zone reminders and reassurance

Sometimes when a young athlete is feeling anxious about an upcoming event, they can be less approachable. If your athlete seems resistant to your questions, here is a strategy you can try:

Parent: How are you feeling about the competition next weekend?

Athlete: Nervous and a bit scared.

Instead of asking more questions at this point, you can offer reassurance using information about their Green Zone experiences.

Parent: It might help to remember what you do when you race your best [in your Green Zone]. You focus on your race plan, you aren't thinking about the time you want to hit. You make your underwaters stronger and push hard off the wall on your turns. That's all you need to do.

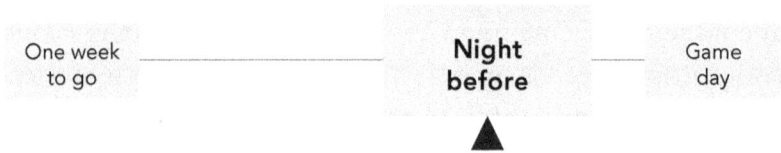

One week to go		**Night before**		Game day

▲

Night before

The evening before the competition starts is usually when parents want to check how their athlete is feeling about the events the next day, if they are prepared, who their opponents will be and discuss a game plan. It seems like a good idea in theory, but most young athletes I work with have indicated that going over these things the night before can make them feel more anxious and question their preparedness. They lie awake in bed going over things in their mind and their sleep is often compromised.

Parents often ask if practising visualisation techniques to rehearse a performance before sleep the night before is a good idea. It is not. Visualising a performance can increase adrenaline and raise the heart rate, preventing the athlete from falling asleep. Mental rehearsal is best done before training or during the day on a consistent basis.

Final preparation checks and discussions about the competition should be taken care of in the week leading up to the event, not the night before. This is good practice, even if your child isn't competing at an elite level. It reinforces the idea that, just like preparation for exams, cramming at the last minute doesn't help. Getting all their gear packed up and ready to go the night before is one preparatory activity that reduces stress. But in general, the night before a major competition should be reserved for relaxation and quiet activities that take the mind off the events of the next day.

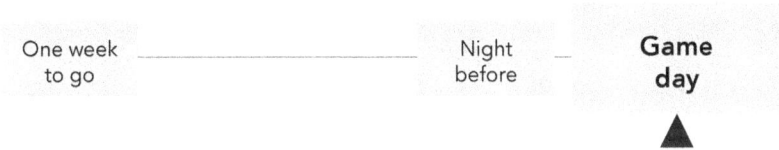

One week to go	Night before	**Game day**

▲

Game Day

By now, most things should be in place, so I'll keep the recommendations for the morning of competition short and sweet.

Dos and don'ts

- Don't be the reason your athlete is late for their warm-up.
- Don't give technical advice or instructions. This increases anxiety and athletes find it distracting.

- Do emphasise the one or two key habits your athlete selected earlier in the week to create a mastery-goal focus.
- 'Just focus on your key habits today, bouncing back from mistakes and positive body language.'
- Do use Green Zone reminders to enhance confidence and control, but keep it brief.
- 'Focus on your race plan, not the time. Strong underwaters and turns. That's all you need to do.'

If you are inclined to, set up reward systems before the game

- Don't establish a reward for solely achieving a certain result, this creates an ego-climate and a results-only focus.
- Do reward key habits, such as giving maximum effort, strong emotional control and supporting others – this creates a mastery-climate. Rewards for attaining a certain result should be a bonus.

QUICK POINTS

- The key message you want to send to your athlete is, 'There is no such thing as perfect preparation.' Being a great competitor is about knowing how to compensate and adjust as you go.
- Setting goals for the results should be done weeks before the competition, not the week before an event.
- The night before a major competition should be reserved for relaxation and quiet activities that take the mind off tomorrow.

CHAPTER 6
DURING THE GAME

Case 7: Resisting support from the sidelines

Ray is 13 years old and loves having his dad at his tennis matches, but he recognises that he doesn't respond well to his father's encouragement from the sidelines when he's playing poorly. It is not uncommon for athletes around this age to experience this. They are aware of it and want to change this pattern of reactions, but often aren't sure how to do this.

Ray explains, 'My dad is really supportive. When he watches my matches he is always encouraging, even if I'm not playing well and I'm down in a match. I'll look over to him and he'll say, "Next point, let's go". Sometimes it's okay, but there are times I've noticed for some reason I get more angry. Instead of agreeing with his comments and moving on, I start talking to my dad in my head. "Did you see what I just did? How can I be calm? That's so bad!" And then I just spiral down.'

I often hear comments like this from young athletes who recognise that their parents are encouraging from the sidelines, but they do not respond to it effectively. Instead of accepting the encouragement, they defy and resist it in their moments of frustration.

Keep it cool

Research conducted with teens participating in tennis has also found that seemingly supportive practices from parents can actually be perceived as pressurising by athletes.

A player in a study by Knight and Holt (2014) explained, 'There can be too much clapping and too much support, trying to will me on. Doesn't she understand that I'm playing as well as I can? I feel too much expectation, she's expecting me to win.'

Above all else, young athletes between the ages of 7 and 14 years do not want their parents to act like *crazed fans* or *demanding coaches* from the sidelines (Omli & Wiese-Bjornstal, 2011). Being a crazed fan includes behaviours such as arguing with the coach or officials, yelling and reacting to bad calls by referees or fanatical cheering. Coaching from the sidelines is as detrimental to a young athlete's performance as the actions of the crazed fan, but much more common in youth sport. Most parents do not realise that when their actions are directive during the game, they can raise feelings of anxiety and pressure in their athletes (Bois, Lalanne & Delforge, 2009). These actions can shift an athlete's focus away from the task at hand and cause them to second guess their movement or play, especially when a parent's instructions are different from those of the coach. Shouting instructions, such as 'get down there' or 'shoot it', correcting technique, or giving advice from the sidelines is confusing, distracting and pressurising. For athletes in team sports, the most commonly mentioned unwanted instruction is to 'pass it' to a teammate. From the young athlete's perspective, it is crucially important that all parents avoid actions that can be disruptive, embarrassing or distracting during the game.

Don't be discouraged by this critique of parent practices in youth sport. It might seem as if the only way forward is to wear a straightjacket to every game, but there are better options, I promise. In my work, I have found that parents are afraid that if they don't shout out a few verbal encouragements or instructions here and there from the sidelines their child might think they don't care or perceive them to be unsupportive. Let this information here be my assurance to you that this is *not* the case. You do not need to do or say as much as you think to show your ultimate support and attention. This brings us back to the *attentive silence* technique that I introduced in chapter 4. This action involves controlling one's emotions and maintaining a positive attitude through nonverbal cues, while quietly paying attention to the match. Demonstrating attentive silence can be one of the most effective ways to show your support from the sidelines, and here's how to set it up.

Signal encouragement

During the game, rather than offering encouragement and instructions verbally, *attentive silence* or *silent encouragement* can be more effective. I recommend sitting down with your child before the competition and coming up with an agreed gesture or signal of encouragement and support. When your athlete has a say in the signals they prefer to see, it raises their accountability to take in the encouragement when they look over to you on the sidelines.

Some of my clients agree on a simple nod and a smile as their preference for silent encouragement, others enjoy creating a signal that serves as a Green Zone reminder. For example, making a tiger claw to remind them to 'move and attack', or looking up to the sky to signal 'heads up, eyes up'. Creating a unique signal or gesture for encouragement with your athlete's input is also a great way to enhance your bond in the sport journey.

Ask for feedback

It is most beneficial in your sport relationship with your child to ask for their feedback about your actions and body language on the sidelines. Parents, coaches and teachers are often unaware of how their reactions and body language affect an athlete's focus and emotions when competing. In the Knight and Holt (2014) study, a teen tennis player said his mother's behaviour could be, 'Embarrassing because she gets so uptight.' Another participant said, 'Sometimes Dad has a really serious face and you're not sure what it means, so it's sometimes really distracting because you're thinking about what he's thinking.' These comments highlight how important it is to find out how your athlete perceives your behaviours during the game and modify your actions to fit your child's need and preferences.

There are always individual differences. Some athlete's prefer clapping and cheering and some would rather attentive silence.

Find a focus

It is an automatic reflex to stand on the sideline and look out for the things your child could improve on and mentally catalogue the mistakes they make during the game. When you show up to a game without a plan for observing your child's performance, it is human nature to focus on the mistakes and imperfections.

When your observations primarily capture mistakes during the game, dissecting errors and what your child *could*, *should* or *would* have done becomes the primary focus of your debriefing after the game. This approach over time will establish a perfectionist mindset, meaning the child focuses more on trying not to make errors in their next competition. This leads to more tentative and cautious movements and a stronger tendency to be indecisive in the game.

The less knowledge you have about your child's sport, the stronger your tendency will be to observe their performance with a focus on spotting weaknesses and mistakes. In order to hone in on the actions that lead to peak performance – the positive behaviours – you need to know what to look out for first. This is when the chart you created in Chapter 1 with the key habits you value in your child's sport, along with Green Zone actions from Chapter 2, all come into play. These are the actions you need to look out for. In this next section, I will show you how to use this information as a tool to elevate your observation and support from the sidelines.

Positive Actions Chart

Refer to the chart from Chapter 1, with the key habits you value in your child's sport. Managing emotions or reactions to errors, maintaining consistent routines and refocusing effectively are all examples of the key habits that support peak performance, in other words, positive behaviours. This information will now go into your Positive Actions Chart.

GO TO Chapter 1 – Process vs results

Think about positive actions or habits as the opposite of mistakes and weaknesses in a game. Mistakes must be minimised and eliminated, but positive actions should be maximised and performed as much as possible. The Positive Actions Chart serves as your reminder to watch out for the key habits during the game, not just the mistakes. Most importantly, the chart allows you to track or note down how often you see these positive behaviours during the game.

The game changer

Using the chart will change your entire view of the game and how you observe your child's performance. Looking for positive actions requires more attentiveness than watching out for the mistakes, but with practice, it can be a game changer. You will see things you couldn't see as clearly before – the actions that drive high performance. Instead of honing in on mistakes and discrepancies, you will be able to capture the actions that matter most in accelerating your child's sport development.

Following is an example of a Positive Actions Chart in soccer/football. You can print out the chart and place it onto a clipboard, or take notes with a copy on your phone or tablet.

Example Positive Actions Chart in soccer/football

Positive actions – key habits	Actions to look out for	Count – number of times you see the corresponding actions
Never giving up – fighting to the finish	Chasing down the ball. Strong defence/man on. Running hard throughout the match regardless of the score.	
Bouncing back from mistakes or set-backs	A deep breath between plays, shaking the body out. Chasing down the ball or defending immediately after an error or interception, instead of stopping/gesturing/or negative comments directed at self.	

Maintaining exceptional focus – maintaining a focus in the present moment and task at hand	Eyes on the play (wide vision), reading the play. Body squared off to the play. Moving into position early.	
Engaging in positive self-talk	Verbal self-encouragement (let's go). Positive actions or gestures toward self (fist pump, clap, thigh tap).	
Encouraging teammates	Positive gestures or verbal comments.	
Maintaining consistent routines	At bench subbing in, stretching, eyes on game, staying active not passive.	
Displaying positive body language and presentation habits	Eyes up, head up, hands off hips, bouncing on toes, staying active.	
Being receptive to feedback and respecting the coach or other authoritative figures	Nodding to the coach's instructions, open body language and eye contact. Executing the coach's instructions/attempting the corrections immediately.	
		Total =

Who benefits most from the Positive Actions Chart?

I designed this tool for parents to use with children between the ages of nine and 13. Young athletes just starting to play competitively benefit most from this chart. I believe the younger, the better. It will help you shape a mastery-focus in yourself and your athlete, right from the beginning.

If your child is experiencing performance anxiety and pressure to perform, this tool is for you. It shapes awareness of the *how* to compete. Both you and your athlete will become more aware of the key actions your child engages when performing at their best (the Green Zone), and see how these things change when performing at their worst (the Red Zone).

If your child is in transition from 'just for fun' to 'more serious' with their sport, this is the time to engage with the Positive Actions Chart. This is the time when scrutiny of mistakes becomes prominent in raising your athlete's standard of performance. When this happens, striving for perfection grows and confidence drops. You have the opportunity to counterbalance this trend with the Positive Actions Chart in your toolbox.

Counterbalance the focus on mistakes

Typical debrief sessions dissect mistakes and direct the athlete's focus to 'what not to do' next time, what to avoid, eliminate, or minimise. It constricts and confines the athlete's mindset in many ways. Most athletes dread this type of debrief, especially when they perform poorly. In contrast, I have found that young athletes welcome a debrief using the Positive Actions Chart, even when they haven't performed well. This is because the chart directs the conversation to what the child 'can do more of', what can be maximised and expanded. It connects with a *can-do* attitude and a growth mindset.

Don't get me wrong, this tool doesn't set you up to be light and fluffy in your support process. It can be highly professional. You can still be a 'hard task master' using this chart and drive high expectations. The difference between this assessment and others is that it allows you to place as much emphasis on the process as on the results, and gives you an opportunity to raise expectations in the process over time.

The information you collect is not the number of mistakes and statistics, such as the number of successful passes for a football player, or split times in races for a swimmer. The information you collect using the chart concerns the habits that can propel the athlete to more successful passes and better split times.

You have numbers and facts to back up your observations, feedback and praise. In particular, your praise will no longer be vague or disingenuous. When using this tool, your feedback and praise will be more specific and measurable.

How to use the Positive Actions Chart

Use a separate chart for each match or game. Collecting between 5 and 10 positive behaviour charts will give you a range of statistics for a variety of performances, ranging from not so good to great performances, and everything in between. Keep in mind, there is a direct link between performing these key habits and overall results. This is important for your child to see, because this is how they will build trust in their game. Trust comes from knowing that when they raise the bar with these habits, they are more likely to see results they can be proud of. This elevates motivation and confidence over time, because your child has a high degree of control over these actions.

As an example, your child may see that a total of 14 positive actions is the current benchmark for a great performance. More distinctly, they can also see that a great performance includes encouraging teammates 5 times, receptivity to feedback five times and bouncing back from errors positively four times. This information is extremely valuable when it comes time to setting goals for their next competition. Rather than being vague with their goal setting, athletes can aim for clear markers such as, 20 positive actions with a stronger focus on fighting spirit and bouncing back from errors.

Benefits of the Positive Actions Chart

- shapes awareness of *how* to perform
- fosters a mastery-climate
- creates awareness of what peak performance looks like to parents, teachers and coaches, and feels like to young athletes

- allows for the setting of measurable goals with a mastery-focus
- provides opportunities for realistic praise that is specific and based on facts.

Can you use the Positive Actions Chart with teen athletes?

While the chart can be a very effective tool to use with young children, athletes aged 13 and above are typically less willing to let parents chart their performance. Some teens are willing if they have experienced using the chart in their younger years. Whatever the case may be, fostering independence with post-match reflection in teen athletes is very important, so do not be disheartened if your teen isn't up for using the Positive Actions Chart. The key to providing optimal support for this age group is to allow your athlete to be more directive in setting up the type of support you provide during the game and what you should look out for from the sidelines. The two key questions you want to understand are:

- what does your athlete want to focus on during the game?
- how can you best support them from the sidelines?

Answers to these questions will give you a clear understanding of your athlete's goals and needs for the game, without you imposing *your* goals or wishes for their game. Your athlete's responses will provide the information you need to be collaborative instead of instructive.

Ask your athlete:

- what would you like me to pay more attention to for this match or be ready to give feedback about?
- what are your goals for this match?
- what would you like to focus on?
- what do you need today, how can I help?
- is there anything in particular you would like me to do?

If your athlete has selected one or two key habits from the chart as part of their goal setting, these are the positive behaviours you should look out for during the game. As your athlete gets older, it becomes more important to ensure your observations and feedback align with their goals and focus for the game.

QUICK POINTS

- Using the Positive Actions Chart as a tool during the game will change your entire view of the game and how you observe your child's performance.
- Instead of honing in on mistakes and discrepancies, you will be able to capture the actions that matter most in accelerating your child's sport development.

CHAPTER 7
AFTER THE GAME

The car ride home is probably the most significant time and place for parents and athletes to communicate in private directly after the game. On paper, the car ride provides the perfect place for you to debrief and review the competition with your child, but in reality, debriefing at this time presents one enormous headache for most parents and athletes. You can shake off the trips home that end in arguments or the silent treatment, but over time, these moments add up, and they can affect your relationship. However, there are ways to turn it around. In this section, I will walk you through the common mistakes parents make and the techniques for debriefing with your child that will strengthen your bond through sport.

What athletes say about the car ride home

'When I don't play well the first thing my parents say when I get in the car is "What happened?". It's so irritating, I don't know what to say.'

'If I do badly in the competition, my parents will keep trying to talk to me about it. They want to go through my matches. But when I play well, they don't really ask about my games, they only ask where I would like to go for dinner.'

'If it looks like I wasn't trying hard enough, then my parents will say things like, "Do you really have the passion for this game? Maybe you should just quit." They say they invest so much time and money and I don't care. I want to do better, I do have passion, I just feel pressure.'

These comments capture the most common scenarios athletes perceive during the car trip home after the game.

A recent study examined parents' and athletes' accounts of the car ride home following competition (Tamminen et al., 2017). Athletes were from a range of sports, between 11 and 16 years of age (the average age was 13 years old). Some athletes expressed that they were just enduring the car ride home or 'waiting it out'.

When talking with me about their performances, athletes often feel that their parents lack empathy and understanding. It is no surprise that athletes commonly try to avoid debriefing by pretending to sleep or listening to music during the car trip. What's more, young athletes perceive that winning and losing influence the nature of debriefing. A study by Elliott & Drummond (2017) found that football players aged between 12 and 13 years perceived more encouraging and supportive feedback when the final score reflected a tight contest. However, in games where the final score reflected a one-sided win or loss, the nature of the debriefing was perceived as being more critical.

Children do enjoy receiving positive comments after competition, particularly if they recognise that they have performed well. Hearing comments such as 'well done', 'good job' and 'good work' make the time after the game satisfying. However, comments that are corrective, critical or negative contribute to feelings of anxiety and dissatisfaction. These feelings tend to be heightened when the young athletes have already recognised that they have performed poorly before they receive any feedback.

Challenges parents face on the car ride home

'It is so hard to talk to him after a race. I feel like I am walking on eggshells. No matter what I say, even a compliment has the potential to upset him.'

'I usually say, "You did this well, but you didn't do that well and this is where you need to improve." It is hard sometimes, but I still think that you need to talk to them about the good and the bad so they know what to improve on.' (Parent's comment in Tamminen et al., 2017)

These statements capture the challenges parents face when trying to communicate with their athlete after the game. If you also feel this tension and difficulty with debriefing on the way home, you are not alone.

I understand that parents view debriefing after the game as an important part of being a sport parent, and although debriefing has the potential to upset children, most sport parents believe it's a necessary exercise to drive improvement and teach valuable life lessons. Debriefing is important. It is a golden opportunity to help your child learn and improve. But the current state of affairs in youth sport clearly shows there is a big mismatch between the intentions parents have with debriefing and the outcomes these talks have on athletes and the parent–athlete relationship.

I'm often asked if a parent's cultural background influences the nature of their debriefing. My answer is no. I do not believe that a parent's cultural background significantly influences debriefing practices after the game. It is not a matter of culture, it is a matter of sport. Sport has its own culture that supersedes ethnicity and cultural background worldwide. The topics of performance and perfection pervade the practices and conversations of coaches, parents and athletes. Perfection is sought through constant improvement to one's technique and the correction of weaknesses and mistakes. This approach to raising performance directly influences the nature of debriefing in sport from youth sport to the elite level. If you want to create different outcomes for your athlete, you have to be willing to do things differently. You have to be ready to go against the grain of the culture in sport that sets a perfectionist approach to debriefing. At present, the approach parents have to debriefing, the challenges they face, and how children feel about debriefing, is the same for all families I work with, regardless of their diverse cultural backgrounds. In line with my observations, the research on debriefing practices across countries in youth sport is telling a similar story.

Here are the most common mistakes parents are making when debriefing on the car ride home and how to fix them:

- power imbalance
- focus on dissecting errors
- the compliment sandwich
- praise in public vs criticise in private.

Mistake 1: Power imbalance

I understand that most parents want their child to engage with them more during the debrief on the car ride home. I know that you would like them to listen more intently, ask questions, and share more about what they are thinking and going through during the game. In reality though, it seems that most parents feel as if they are talking to a brick wall.

Drawing on theories of power, conflict resolution and communication styles, a brick wall is built between a parent and an athlete, or a coach and an athlete, when a power imbalance exists in communication. This occurs when the communication is one-sided and directed almost exclusively by the adult. If you find your athlete is often disengaged in the interaction, confrontational, or frequently attempts to avoid debrief discussions on the trip home, it is highly likely there is an imbalance of power in the communication.

Following are the most common ways parents establish a power imbalance in debriefing during the car ride home.

- **Overly directive and instructive** – Similar to the traditional style of debriefing in sport, this approach creates a one-sided debriefing process. Parents or coaches do most of the talking and the athlete sits and listens. Parents share their observations and give instructions on how to improve, while the athlete participates very little in the debriefing process. It is extremely difficult for you to gauge what they are thinking and how they are feeling.
- **Using rhetorical questions** – These types of questions are asked in order to create a dramatic effect or to make a point, rather than to get an answer. This approach usually crops up when you are trying to convey your feelings of frustration or disappointment. Common rhetorical questions are, 'what was that?', 'how hard is it to pass the ball?', 'why are you wasting my time?'.
- **Asking leading questions** – Similar to rhetorical questions, the goal of leading questions is to make a point (e.g., 'Do you think it's a good idea to sit cold in the bleachers without your tracksuit on between races?'). There is a right answer and it is intended to make your athlete 'think' about their actions. If the answer to your question is particularly obvious, it will lead to an unresponsive athlete.
- **Repeating or rephrasing points** – You are more likely to do this when the debrief is one-sided, because it's difficult to be sure your athlete is listening and understands what you are saying when they aren't participating in the conversation. You repeat and rephrase to make sure they get it, but this can come across as condescending rather than constructive.

- **Correcting your athlete's responses** – A huge part of the debrief process is about capturing your athlete's experience and perceptions to build their awareness of their Red Zone and Green Zone. It should be a sharing exercise as much as it is a feedback process. When you correct your child's responses, they are less likely to tell you the truth about their experience. This reinforces the perception that there is always a right way and a wrong way, which isn't the case when describing an individual experience. Your athlete will tell you what you want to hear, and they will not share their authentic experience of the game.

Try this – if you would like your child to participate in the debrief and share more about their experiences during the game, the debrief or discussion has to be a bidirectional or two-way process. Creating a two-way debriefing process involves equal input from you and your athlete, which is how you balance power in communication. You set this up by asking questions about your athlete's experience before you give any feedback. No more leading or rhetorical questions. Ask questions with genuine interest and curiosity, so you not only increase your athlete's awareness of their Performance Process, but your own awareness too. When you allow curious questions to lead the way, the tone of your debrief will change from interrogative to supportive and collaborative. You do not need to be overly directive or instructive. Remember your athlete is resourceful and they have inherent tools and solutions inside their Green Zone experiences. Ask questions to draw these out and build awareness of how your child competes at their best.

Mistake 2: Focus on dissecting errors

Going through the mistakes made during the game and ways to fix or improve them is seen as the most important part of debriefing, if not the *only* exercise in the debriefing process. Parents justify negative feedback in the interests of performance improvement. This practice stems from the belief that debriefing is about improving the child's performance, and the best way to do this is to fix a person's weaknesses and eliminate their errors. This approach builds situational awareness and strategic knowledge, but it does not shape a confident and resilient athlete. For this, you need to help them to develop their positive behaviours and key habits in the game.

The more you focus on the assessment of errors, the more anxious your child will be, and the more they will focus on trying not to make errors in their next game. According to research on debriefing with this approach (Elliott & Drummond, 2017), children may even avoid performing particular skills and actions in their next match.

Alternative approach 1:
Using the Positive Actions Chart

Do not focus solely on going over mistakes and how to fix them in your debrief after the competition. I firmly believe that you don't need to go over mistakes at all, especially if you know how to systematically debrief the things that elevate confidence, enjoyment and performance. You can do this by looking into the execution of key habits or positive behaviours. If you are using the Positive Actions Chart, you will see a drop in these actions, if your athlete did not perform well. When you debrief in this way, you focus on the factors your athlete has a high degree of control over. More importantly, these are the actions your athlete can 'do more of' instead of avoiding or trying to 'do less of' in their next event.

Following is an example debrief between a parent and athlete using the Positive Actions Chart.

Example: Positive Action Chart debrief in soccer/football

Positive Actions Key habits	Actions to look out for	Count
Never giving up fighting to the finish	Chasing down the ball. Strong defence/man on. Running hard throughout the match regardless of the score.	ⲎⲎⲦ
Bouncing back from mistakes or set-backs	A deep breath between plays, shaking the body out. Chasing down the ball or manning up immediately after an error or interception, instead of stopping/gesturing/engaging in negative comments directed at self.	I
Maintaining exceptional focus – in the present moment and task at hand	Eyes on the play (wide vision), reading the play, body squared off to the play, moving into position early.	III
Employing positive self-talk	Verbal self-encouragement (lets go), positive actions or gestures toward self (fist pump, clap, thigh tap).	I
Encouraging teammates	Positive gestures or verbal comments.	0
Maintaining consistent routines	At bench, subbing in – stretching, eyes on game, staying active not passive.	0
Displaying positive body language and presentation habits	Eyes up, head up, hands off hips, bouncing on toes, staying active.	I

Being receptive to feedback and respecting the coach or other authoritative figures	Nodding to the coach's instructions, open body language and eye contact. Executing the coach's instructions/attempting the corrections immediately.	II
		Total = 13

Parent: 'I didn't see your key habits as much today as I did in your last top performance. I could see you were trying to **focus on the ball** and moving into position. **Bouncing back from mistakes** and your **communication with your team-mates** was lower today.'

'Do you agree? What did you notice in yourself today?'

Athlete: 'I let the **mistakes affect me** today, and my **body language** slumped. I was **trying to focus** on the game, but I needed to **be more positive** in my head and with my team. This is what I will try to do better in the next game.'

Alternative approach 2: Building awareness of the Red Zone and Green Zone

Instead of going over the mistakes, build awareness of your athlete's Performance Process by reviewing Green Zone and Red Zone moments. I introduced key questions in Chapter 2, and I present them here again as a way to build a conversational approach to debriefing. These questions will allow your athlete to understand how they contribute to the ups and downs in their performance, and what they can lean into or focus on more strongly next time to improve.

GO TO Chapter 2 – Key questions to build awareness

Capturing the Green Zone

When you were *having fun and felt happiest* in the game today...

- how did you approach your game?
- what did your movements and technique feel like?
- what did you do between points or plays when things were going well today?
- what were you thinking about or focused on?
- what were you saying to yourself?

Capturing the Red Zone

When your felt annoyed, frustrated or down today…
- did your actions change?
- what was different?
- what did your movements and technique feel like?
- were there actions you stopped doing?
- what was your reaction to your errors or mistakes like?

Alternative approach 3: Preventing mistakes vs reactive solutions

When you discuss ways to fix the mistakes made in a game with your athlete, you typically discuss the technical or tactical solutions. Sometimes these solutions could be counter to the coach's instructions, or just repeating the same things. Either way, no matter how experienced you are in your child's sport, if you want them to have a good relationship with their coach, you should let the coach be the authority on tactics and technique.

There is another way you can help your athlete work through mistakes. For instance, when you focus on fixing errors with tactical and technical knowledge, you build the *what* or the *how* to improve situational responses. This information forms the *solutions* for managing similar scenarios in the next competition. This is the important job of the coach in debriefing.

As a parent, you can help your athlete be more aware of the *preventions* rather than the solutions. Instead of focusing on tactical and technical solutions, you can help your athlete understand what they were focused on, thinking about, and what they were actually doing at the time they made an error. You will help them build awareness of the *why* behind the mistakes they made. This approach is most useful with teen athletes who compete in an elite sport environment. We can't deny that dissecting errors will be a big part of their processes in this environment. But when you discuss prevention plans using information from the Red Zone and Green Zone, you can offer a complimentary perspective.

Emphasising prevention plans

- **Step 1: Understand the *why*** – Ask your athlete about the *why*. 'When you went off track in the game and you made a few errors in a row, can you recognise what you were focused on at the time?', 'What you were thinking about?', 'How did your actions change?'
- **Step 2: Prevention plan using the Green Zone** – Next, bring the emphasis to their Green Zone thoughts and actions and the positive behaviours. Ask your athlete, 'When you were performing well today, what were you thinking about?', 'How did you feel?', 'What did you do on the pitch and in between plays?'

Your athlete's response to these questions will be included in the *prevention plan*. Learning from mistakes in this way is empowering for the athlete because it focuses on how they can be proactive in managing their game, *not* just reactive to mistakes. What's more, circling back to using their Green Zone habits will raise confidence and enjoyment in their next game.

Mistakes 3: The compliment sandwich

Parents typically approach debriefing with a technique described as a 'compliment sandwich'. This approach involves a sandwich of comments beginning with a series of positive comments, followed by one or two critical comments and concluding with a final positive comment.

Professors Elliot and Drummond (2017) studied the debriefing practices of parents with young athletes in Australian football, and found that most parents viewed the compliment sandwich as an easy 'go to' approach for debriefing and a conservative one for that matter.

The sandwich approach offers an easy way to structure the delivery of your feedback, starting with praise to enhance the athlete's receptiveness to feedback, then delivering critical comments that capture and note the mistakes made that day. A compliment then concludes the feedback process, to finish on a positive note.

When you apply the sandwich technique as your 'go to' feedback strategy over many seasons, there is a tendency to become vaguer in the delivery of positive comments and more specific with critical comments over time. I hear parents say, 'You've done some great things today, but your footwork wasn't great', 'You did this in the first quarter, and that in the second half, but overall good job today.'

The compliment sandwich doesn't hide criticism or negative feedback. Just as parents are prone to putting a spotlight on mistakes, children do the same when receiving the compliment sandwich. Over time, when your positive remarks are vaguer, the athlete's attention will be drawn to the specific criticisms and dismiss the compliments.

The compliment sandwich is a one-sided debriefing approach. Praise tends to be vague and criticism is usually more specific. The only advantage to the compliment sandwich is its consistent, structured delivery. Here is an alternative approach, which is also highly systematic but creates a collaborative atmosphere. Instead, try Good–Better–How.

Good–Better–How

Good–Better–How is a simple three-question debriefing system. The questions ensure that you gather feedback from your athlete first. Your role is to guide your athlete to be more specific with their answers and offer suggestions or brainstorm the *how* to improve for training.

- **Good**: three things you did well?
- **Better**: one thing you can improve?
- **How**: how will you go about doing this in your next training session?

Starting with the *good* (three things you did well) brings awareness to the positive behaviours and habits performed. This question isn't about the results, it is to tap into the habits your athlete did well in their Performance Process and Green Zone moments.

It can be difficult to choose *only* one thing to improve, but this is crucial for initiating action. When an athlete has too many things to work on, they don't work on anything at all. This step gives them the opportunity to be clear and specific about what to improve.

The *how* step empowers your athlete to take ownership of their progress instead of waiting for you or their coach to tell them what to do. You can offer, suggest or help your athlete brainstorm how they will work on things in training.

Mistakes 4: Praise in public vs criticise in private

Both parents and athletes in the study by Tamminen and colleagues (2017) reported that praise and positive feedback were given most often in front of other parents after the game, and critical feedback was reserved for private conversations. The timing and the privacy afforded by the car ride home provides the opportunity for more serious talks. However, if your debriefs are predominately critical in nature, athletes anticipate the car ride home to be a fairly miserable experience. This is amplified in athletes who perform poorly, causing them to either 'wait it out' or 'block out' your comments. The conversation will only become more one-sided and you will find it hard to break through the wall that you have built in the process.

It appears that the degree of criticism and negative feedback can change depending on who is in the car. Studies have found that when mums or teammates are in the car, the feedback is less critical and the conversation focuses mainly on things that the athlete did well. I have found that athletes appreciate the positive feedback directly after a match, but when there is a disparity between the feedback from mum (often being more positive) and dad (often being more critical), athletes start to question the genuineness of the positive comments. I often hear comments such as 'is it real or is my mum just saying that to make me feel better?' I believe athletes, as young as eight years old, appreciate genuine, positive feedback based on the facts. It is valuable for mums and dads to be on the same page with the debrief approach, and it is possible using the techniques I have highlighted in this chapter.

Critical thinking

'It's not about the result or the mistakes. If she loses to her opponent but I know she tried her best, then I will be proud. But what I cannot accept is her bad attitude, giving up, like she doesn't care and she doesn't even try. This is what I get upset about.'

This is a valid position parents and coaches often share with me, and I understand how it relates to the key habits you value in your child's sport. But before you express your frustration with your athlete's behaviour in competition, consider this point first: have you done your homework?

Before you express your frustration and your overt criticism, you need to ask yourself if you've done your part to shape a mastery-climate. Remember, there is always an explanation for behaviour, even a lack of action. All children innately want to please their parents and coach by performing well in competition. When an athlete looks like they couldn't care less, aren't following the game plan, or are giving up (especially when told they're talented), these actions are the by-product of an ego-focus, which is established by the ego-climate you shape.

You have to do your homework and work to build a mastery-climate. Have the conversations and do the exercises to emphasise the process as much as the results. An athlete with a mastery-focus will lean into executing the key habits, regardless of the score, especially when they are behind in a game.

You will come across as being overly critical when:

- your debriefing focuses primarily on the dissection of mistakes
- you have a strong ego-focus and your child has performed poorly
- you have high expectations for the results and low expectations for the Performance Process
- you have not discussed mastery-focused goals with your athlete.

You can conduct a highly professional debrief *without criticism* when:

- you use the Positive Actions Chart
- you discuss mastery-focused goals, such as bouncing back from errors quickly and showing positive body language in the next game
- you explore Red Zone and Green Zone moments with feedback from your athlete
- you ask questions to create a two-way conversation.

My vision is for you to shape conversations and debriefs after the game that bring you and your child closer in the sport journey, form insights together that inspire, and build belief in the Performance Process. The strategies I've introduced in this chapter can shape a positive debrief regardless of the outcome your athlete faces, because every technique focuses on the Performance Process and emphasises a mastery-focus.

Best way to convey empathy

A final note on empathy. As your athlete moves into their late teens, showing empathy and understanding becomes very important. The key is to read your athlete's emotional state in relation to the outcome of the game. You don't have to walk on eggshells, you just need to talk about the most difficult outcomes your child might face and how they would like you to support them.

Difficult outcomes might be:

- losing by a big margin
- a great performance with a loss
- losing a final match with a nail-biting finish.

Following a difficult outcome, some athletes prefer to debrief once they reach home; it's a timing issue. Others prefer to release all their frustrations during the trip home; then they are ready to move on once they reach home. I know some athletes who only want to talk about their Green Zone after a great performance with a loss. There are a few who will stick with the Good-Better-How review no matter the outcome. Taking into account your athlete's emotional state and adapting to their needs are the most significant ways to convey your support, empathy and understanding.

QUICK POINTS

- Move away from asking rhetorical or leading questions in your discussions after the game. *Asking questions with genuine interest* and curiosity will change the tone of your debrief from interrogative to supportive and collaborative.
- *Do not focus solely on going over mistakes* in your debrief after the game. Use the Positive Actions Chart to explore the actions your athlete can 'do more of' instead of avoid or 'do less of' in their next event.
- If you do talk about mistakes, instead of focusing on the tactical and technical solutions, *explore prevention plans using Green Zone habits.* Help your child to be proactive in managing their game, not just reactive.

CHAPTER 8

THE PERFECTIONIST ATHLETE AND THE PERFECTIONIST PARENT

Year on year, I see an increasing number of young athletes struggling with the perils of perfectionism. This aligns with recent research that has shown a significant rise in perfectionist striving in society in the last decade (Curran & Hill, 2019). Perfectionist athletes can be labelled as the ones who can't handle the pressure of competing, find it hard to take on technical corrections, and panic when there are sudden changes in the plan. I hear coaches and parents say, 'Maybe sport isn't for this child. It might be best to do other things that aren't so stressful.' I understand the difficulties in supporting a perfectionist athlete. However, if you use this approach to solve the problem, especially when considering that perfectionism is on the rise, you might not have many athletes to coach in the future! Parents, teachers and coaches can come to understand perfectionism in young athletes on a deeper level and be armed with support strategies that will help them to thrive.

Most people think a perfectionist is someone who has very high standards in all things they do, who doesn't like things out of place, and who wants everything they do to be 'just right', or in other words, 'perfect'. This describes the broad, hallmark qualities of a perfectionist, but it doesn't provide the full picture. Perfectionism is far more complex than just 'striving for perfection'. Coaches, parents and teachers often don't realise that the difficulties their athletes are going through are due to perfectionism, because they are missing a big chunk of what it entails. In fact, many families are surprised to learn that their athlete's curious style of thinking and habits are part and parcel of being a perfectionist. In this chapter, I will show you the full picture of perfectionism and help you understand the idiosyncrasies of the young perfectionist in sport.

Perfectionism is a topic that I am very passionate about. My research during my masters and doctorate degrees focused on the study of perfectionism in sport and exercise (Longbottom, J.-L., Grove, J. R. & Dimmock, J. A., 2012; Longbottom, J-L., Grove, J. R. & Dimmock, J. A., 2010). The question I wanted to answer was, 'Is perfectionism in sport and exercise pursuits good, bad, or both?' My research findings revealed that perfectionist qualities are not all bad, neither are they all good. Perfectionism is both good and bad. There are some perfectionist qualities that energise action and form the bright side of perfectionism. There is also another group of qualities that can be highly destructive and form the dark side of perfectionism.

Over the past 15 years I have moved from researching perfectionism to directly supporting perfectionist athletes in my private practice. It is like supporting a live performance from backstage in the wings, and then watching it from front-row seats. The backstage view is the research behind perfectionism. I studied the key features of the traits, the mechanics and how the working parts fit together. Now in private practice, I witness how athletes experience these traits, front and centre. I see the complexities of perfectionism in young athletes *and* their parents, in ways that are not well documented or discussed. Young athletes show signs of perfectionism very early, but they can also be good at hiding some of the common quirks. I want to help you see the full picture of being a perfectionist, both the bright and the dark side.

I refer to the bright side as *striving perfectionism* and the dark side as *strained perfectionism*.

- **The strained perfectionist** perceives a great deal of pressure from parents and coaches to achieve a perfect performance. Doubts about their ability and a concern over mistakes are defining characteristics of this dark side.
- **The striving perfectionist** is self-driven and strives to achieve high standards with an intense work ethic and an affinity for neatness and precision.

By the end of this chapter, you will be able to read the signs of perfectionism in your athlete *and* yourself. Most importantly, you will be ready to encourage your athlete to harness the brighter side of being a perfectionist and keep the dark side in check as the young athlete grows.

Let's take a closer look at the ingredients that distinguish the bright side and the dark side of perfectionism, so you can better recognise the key features.

The dark side –
strained perfectionism

Athletes who fit this profile have a strong need to avoid disapproval from others. They worry extensively about what their parents, coach or teachers will think if they don't perform well, which is why they seek reassurance often. This people pleasing and worrying about others' expectations creates a lot of anxiety on the dark side of perfectionism. Young athletes who represent the strained perfectionist strongly believe they *must not* make errors in order to perform well. So when they compete it's no surprise that they focus intensely on trying not to make errors, are prone to being cautious and don't take risks during the game. The strained perfectionist rarely enjoys competing because of the anguish they go through to prepare. Typically, their thoughts are cluttered with a great deal of self-doubt in the form of 'What ifs' (e.g., 'What if I mess this up?'), and concern over mistakes because they are aiming for error-free performances. Immense self-criticism and disappointment following a poor performance maintain a strong fear of failure. Going over and over mistakes in one's mind and taking a long time to move on from disappointing experiences is an unfortunate tendency. This unhelpful pattern of reflection is one of the strongest contributors to the strain on the dark side of perfectionism.

Defining qualities of strained perfectionism

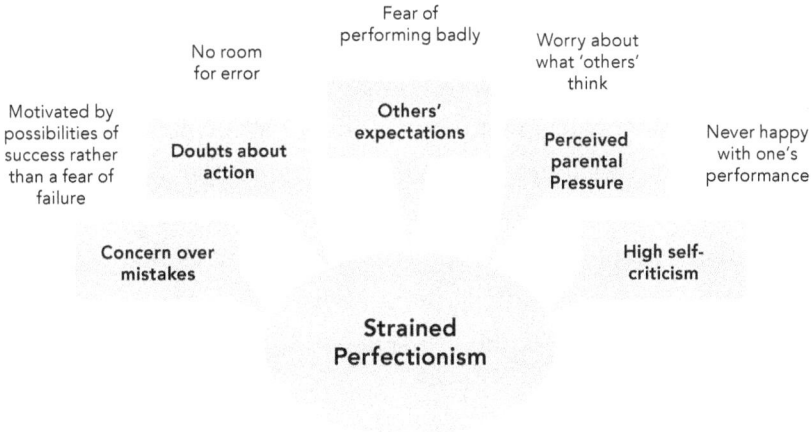

Fear of
performing badly

No room
for error

Worry about
what 'others'
think

Motivated by
possibilities of
success rather
than a fear of
failure

**Doubts about
action**

**Others'
expectations**

**Perceived
parental
Pressure**

Never happy
with one's
performance

**Concern over
mistakes**

**High self-
criticism**

**Strained
Perfectionism**

The young athlete who represents the Strained Perfectionist would strongly agree with these statements:

- if I can't do something perfectly then there is no point even trying
- I should be upset if I make a mistake
- the better I do, the better I am expected to do
- I rarely give myself credit when I do well because there's always something I could have done better.

Case 8: The young strained perfectionist in sport

Brian is a 13-year-old football player who comes to my office with his father after experiencing a run of disappointing performances. Brian made the step to play more competitively about two years ago and in the past six months he hasn't been progressing, despite an increasing number of training hours.

Brian's dad says, 'He seems to be losing confidence and overall is really stressed and unhappy a lot of the time. Brian is talented with so much potential but I feel he doesn't see it.'

In the days leading up to competitions he is known to get into a panic and has meltdowns. His father explains that the family want to support Brian if he wants to play competitive football, but they are becoming increasingly concerned about his mental wellbeing and feel that if it continues this way, he might be better off putting his time into other things. At the same time, he worries the problems will just transfer to other activities.

Brian's father says, 'We feel that if there is an opportunity for him to learn to alter his mindset then it could be valuable for life beyond sport.'

When Brian and I assess his experience, he explains that he worries a lot about letting his parents and coach down and feels that everyone is watching him and expecting him to perform well. On the pitch, he feels like he is overthinking everything, 'Should I do this, or that?' He is indecisive and that leads to a lot of unusual mistakes. Sometimes he feels tired and unmotivated and the first thought that comes to his mind is, what is the point? When this happens, he wants to be alone and doesn't want to talk to anyone. He ends up doing nothing, procrastinating on homework and everything piles up.

In Brian's case you can sense how stressed and strained he is due to the perception that other people expect him to perform *perfectly*. Brian believes strongly that the *better he does, the better he is expected to do.* Feelings of intense anxiety and pressure are present because of the way strained perfectionists like Brian define what it means to perform well. In Brian's mind, a great performance is an error-free game, which is in no way necessary, realistic, or even rational.

With their rigid and irrational way of viewing high performance, strained perfectionists have an avoidance focus when competing. Instead of striving to win, they compete to *avoid* losing, and *not* let others down. Instead of focusing on giving their full effort and trying their best, they focus on avoiding or trying *not* to make errors. When a young athlete's inner dialogue is full of 'the don'ts' (e.g., 'don't hit it out'), instead of 'the do's' (e.g., 'I will hit it there!'), worries and doubts about their ability will follow, and strain is imminent. Without positive conviction in mind, indecisive action when competing is a typical tendency.

What's the point? Interestingly, this is one very specific thought that I hear often from both young and adult strained perfectionists. This thought comes up when the strain leads to fatigue and depletes motivation. The strain turns to drain when the doubts about their action and ability take over, sometimes in the form of questions that clutter the mind. 'What will others think?' and 'Am I good enough?', coupled with rigid expectations, such as 'If I am going to do something, I'd better do it right or perfect the first time!' This pattern of thought sends the strained perfectionist running for the hills and they will usually withdraw, procrastinate, or sit idle. If this pattern of thought and action occurs often enough, young athletes can get branded as unmotivated, lazy, unwilling to try, or being someone who don't care. It is the strained perfectionism at work here, not simply a child who lacks drive.

The bright side – striving perfectionism

This is the type of perfectionism that society praises, and the world of elite sport glorifies in our Olympic champions. Therefore, it is the type of perfectionism that people recognise most easily. Young athletes who exemplify the striving perfectionist are highly self-focused, and they take the initiative to set their own goals, rather than waiting for others to prescribe them. The key words in this profile are 'striving' and 'personal.' They aim high and take their goals seriously, without needing much input from coaches or parents. In fact, their expectations are typically higher than the expectations parents, coaches or teachers have for them. When the striving perfectionist is confident and passionate about their sport, they can pursue their goals with tunnel vision, drive and persistence. The striving perfectionist doesn't require a lot of push from others. Parents and coaches will say *they* are the ones who need to tell their athlete it's time to stop training or studying and switch off for the day.

The striving perfectionist is known to have a strong work ethic. Young athletes with this trait are typically described by their coaches as the ones that give 120% in training most of the time, setting them up to be great role models and the first choice for team captains.

The third component of striving perfectionism is a need for organisation, neatness and precision. This quality leads to meticulous action and conscientiousness in the tasks they take on. Young athletes with this trait are meticulous with their routines for competition preparation. In training they are diligent and aim for top precision with their technique.

Defining qualities of striving perfectionism

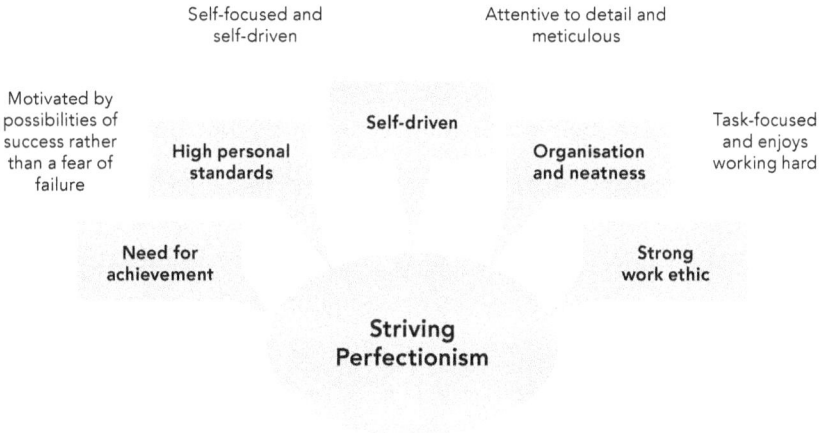

Self-focused and
self-driven

Attentive to detail and
meticulous

Motivated by
possibilities of
success rather
than a fear of
failure

Self-driven

Task-focused
and enjoys
working hard

**High personal
standards**

**Organisation
and neatness**

**Need for
achievement**

**Strong
work ethic**

**Striving
Perfectionism**

The young athlete who represents the Striving Perfectionist would strongly agree with these statements:

- I strive to be the best at everything I do
- neatness and organisation are important to me
- I would say I am hardworking in everything I set out to do
- when I make plans, I follow through with them.

You can sense the drive and persistence that comes from these affirmations. The qualities that define striving perfectionism clearly have the power to energise action in a young athlete. Interestingly, recent research has concluded that when these qualities are working positively and productively together, it looks almost the same as 'conscientiousness', and suggest this to be a more fitting label to describe this trait. I agree wholeheartedly with this perspective. When working with a young striving perfectionist athlete, I introduce strategies to harness these qualities and use them intelligently and strategically, so that the child's conscientiousness, work ethic and pride in their efforts can shine through. When the striving perfectionist is at their best, they aim high, but they can also reflect on their performance and mistakes productively, especially when they do not achieve the desired result. Positive striving occurs when the perfectionist can be highly task-focused rather than focused only on the results. Building high expectations on performing the key habits in their process and valuing their process as much as they do the results is crucial. When this occurs, the striving perfectionist is fiercely focused on the task at hand and operates with tunnel vision on their goals. Drawing on the learnings from the previous chapters, you could say this profile looks a lot like a young athlete who is highly conscientious with a strong mastery-climate focus.

When one side is strong the other side is weak

Keep in mind that a perfectionist will have both the bright and dark sides of perfectionism. When one side appears to be more prominent, the other side will be weaker and less significant. Another way to picture it is, when one side is high the other side is low. For example, when strained perfectionism is *high* a young athlete will be experiencing intense doubts about their ability and concern over mistakes. In turn, striving perfectionism will be *low,* such that the positive striving with intense focus and strong work ethic will be diminished.

The bridge between the bright side and the dark side

When a young striving perfectionist becomes totally inflexible and unrealistic with their expected outcomes, they will start to think 'have I done enough?' when prepping for competition. Over time, when they keep failing to reach their rigid expectations, they will become more self-critical, and when preparing their main thought turns into 'Am I good enough?' Doubts about their actions and ability surge, giving rise to strained perfectionism. This shift in thinking is the bridge leading from the bright side to the dark side of perfectionism. This doesn't happen overnight, it takes time, but when it does, an athlete that once fit more closely with the profile of the striving perfectionist will look more like a strained perfectionist.

The bridge from the Bright Side (Striving Perfectionism) to the Dark Side (Strained Perfectionism)

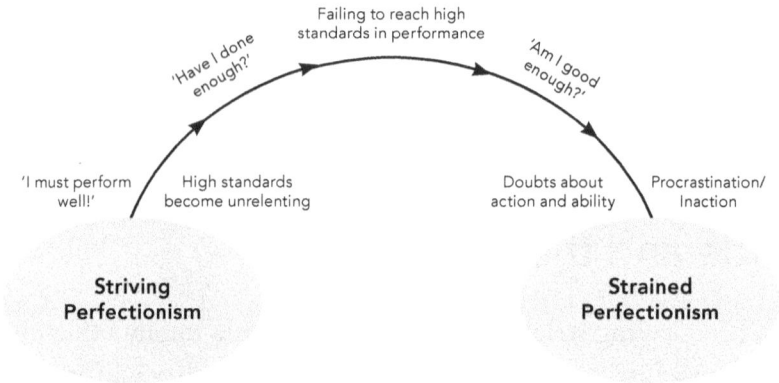

Failing to reach high standards in performance

'Have I done enough?'

'Am I good enough?'

'I must perform well!'

High standards become unrelenting

Doubts about action and ability

Procrastination/ Inaction

Striving Perfectionism

Strained Perfectionism

Spinning into over-drive

Now you know that striving perfectionism can be positive for young athletes when they remain task-focused, take pride in their efforts, and process missed targets productively. However, when the perfectionist doesn't know when to stop, and their expectations become rigid, with a results-only focus, the striving can unfortunately lead to extremes. An athlete's passion for sport can become obsession and their strong work ethic can lead to overdoing it and losing sight of boundaries. When everything spins into overdrive, striving perfectionism can shift from being positive to being problematic in young athletes.

Case 9: When the young striving perfectionist overdoes it

Sam is a 15-year-old swimmer and came by my office with his mum for his first session. Sam's mum began our team chat by describing her son's achievements.

'In the past few years Sam has become one of the top swimmers in his club,' she said. 'He is very competitive and hardworking, and he is the type of child who wakes up early on his days off of his own accord to do extra conditioning. We have never put any pressure on Sam to perform well or do more than asked of him by his coach, he's just always been quite diligent.'

But over the course of the previous six months, things had grown increasingly out of hand. Sam had been overdoing it with extra workouts, leading to an overuse injury, and he had started to become more restrictive about what he was eating. Sam had the opportunity to train overseas during the summer holidays, which the family thought would be a great booster for his performance. But for some reason, ever since he returned, he seems to be training harder than ever but sliding backwards in performance.

Sam's mum said, 'Maybe Sam needs to learn to train smarter not harder, I'm not sure.'

During the session, Sam explained that since he started performing well, he has felt more pressure to keep it that way.

'I feel like I must do well,' he said.

I could see that Sam's preparation for meets had also become more demanding.

He said, 'I started taking my preparation the week before meets more seriously, eating the right things, and getting more sleep, but I seem to be more tense on race day. In training, I try to focus hard on my technique, but it doesn't feel right most of the time and I get frustrated.'

Sam thought it would be important to mention that he noticed some of his superstitious habits had increased too.

'My coach says I care too much, and I need to have more fun. The harder I work, the worse I get. I don't know where to go from here.'

Positive striving first

At the beginning of this case description, you can see the bright side of the striving perfectionist in action. The qualities of the self-focused, diligent, quiet achiever are evident in Sam's case. When there are no explicit expectations on the results, the striving perfectionist enjoys working hard toward their goals and steady progress keeps reinforcing their work ethic. They seem more passionate than obsessive about their sport. You can see the conscientious athlete with a strong mastery-focus in action.

Raising the stakes

The harder Sam works, the more he raises his expectations on the results. Working hard and investing more becomes a reason to raise expectations. Unfortunately, specialised training opportunities also raise the expectations Sam has of himself to perform well. When expectations become unrelenting, positive striving turns into demanding thoughts and pressure (e.g., 'I have to' do well). And when these expectations are not met, the response is to work harder still. In Sam's case, the extra effort and hard work are focused on controlling and perfecting his preparation and his technique. This approach to self-improvement won't build the confidence and control the perfectionist is looking for. It can only lead to more anxiety because their habits and actions become more rigid, trying to get everything 'just right'; to be perfect.

One of the hardest problems to witness in perfectionists is highly unproductive perspectives about special training opportunities like Sam's overseas training stint. I hear young athletes like Sam say, 'My family have invested so much in me, and I know I have worked hard, so I expect myself to perform well.' This could be positively conscientious if the athlete is referring to performing the positive actions and key habits in their process more strongly. But it isn't productive or positive in this case because the expectations the athlete is referring to are about the results and *only* the results. What's more, the expectations are not only vague (e.g., to do well and be perfect), but also unrelenting. For you, the parents and coaches, I completely understand how heartbreaking and infuriating this can be.

I hear parents say, 'How can this happen? We do what we can to support our children, and we just want to give them the opportunities, not for them to feel pressured or burdened by it.' There is a way to fix this dilemma. I'll show you in the next section of this chapter, and it does not involve revoking your investment or support.

The need for control

One behaviour that perfectionists try to keep under wraps is their superstitious habits around their sport. Common types of superstitions are eating particular foods for breakfast before competing, wearing a lucky pair of underwear or socks, placing equipment in a specific place, and quirky actions such as tapping the top of the doorframe before leaving the house on race day. When high standards become unrelenting, passion turns into obsession and the striving perfectionist looks for more and more ways to feel in control or find control over their performance. This is how superstitious habits that were small quirks and rituals in preparation for competition get out of hand. This experience can become scary for athletes and their families as they notice they are losing control whilst trying hard to find control.

Superstitious habits can increase and then become more compulsive when young athletes feel stress, pressure and anxiety. One example of this pattern is switching the light off before leaving the house to head to the pool. Initially this action could have been part of the typical routine before leaving home, but suddenly it becomes a ritual of switching the light on and off again 20 times before leaving the house for competition.

Now, if you are thinking, wait, this sounds a lot more like obsessive compulsive disorder (OCD) than perfectionism to me, you could be right. At the extreme end of the spectrum, striving perfectionism is linked to OCD. It is important to be mindful that this information should not lead you to diagnosing your child with clinical issues or to using the strategies presented in this chapter to treat any clinical problems. It is important to seek professional support if you notice this behaviour. I have included this information here so you are aware of the full picture of perfectionism – the dark side, the bright side, and what happens when striving perfectionism pushes to extremes. In doing so, I want you to feel empowered with the insights, to understand perfectionism better, and be ready to respond if you see these things in your young athlete.

Common actions and habits of perfectionists

Positive actions:
- striving perfectionism gives rise to conscientiousness, fearsome focus and effort.

Negative actions:
- strained perfectionism gives rise to avoidance, seclusion and inaction
- striving perfectionism gives rise to overdoing things, overcorrecting and controlling.

The Red Zone and Green Zone experience for young perfectionists

In chapter 2, I introduced the concepts of the Red Zone and Green Zone to help you understand an athlete's Performance Process.

GO TO Chapter 2 – A closer look at the Red Zone and Green Zone

As a reminder:

- **The Red Zone leads to poor performance.** In this zone, athletes experience negative emotions, and their thoughts and actions are ineffective.
- **The Green Zone leads to peak performance.** In this zone, athletes experience positive emotions, and their thoughts and actions are productive.

I think it's valuable for you to see what a young perfectionist experiences in their sport when they are in the Red Zone and the Green Zone. You will observe the typical thoughts, feelings and actions from the dark side of perfectionism inside the athlete's Red Zone. In contrast, the Green Zone is full of highly productive and powerful thoughts and actions. In the Green Zone, you will be able to see the bright side of perfectionism shining through. I am always inspired to see this when I do the analysis with a young perfectionist, and I know you will be too!

The Red Zone in a young perfectionist athlete

Thoughts/ Focus	Feelings	Actions
Have I done enough? Am I good enough?	Anxious Scared	Hesitant and cautious with my movements
Trying not to make a mistake	Tired Unmotivated	Focused on my technique, trying to get it right
Indecision – is this right? Should I do this, or that?		I don't want to talk to anyone. Want to shut myself away
In response to errors – I'll never be good enough I'm so stupid What's the point?		Giving up Don't do anything

Doubts about action and abillity →

Concern over mistakes →

Trying to get everything 'just right' / perfect leads to indecisiveness →

Self=criticism is high. Giving up on self →

← Trying to find control

← Withdrawing and non-communicative

Quittting and inaction

The Green Zone in a young perfectionist athlete

Thoughts/Focus	Feelings	Actions
I can do this!	Confident	More aggressive
Thinking about the future and all the things I can achieve	Proud	Going for it
	Focused	My movements are stronger and more powerful
	Motivated	
Focused on myself		
Focused on what I have to do, on the small tasks		I keep pushing when I'm tired, I don't give up
		Talkative and communicate more
Response to errors: It's OK, I can work it out		

Positive self-talk and optimism

Highly task-focused

Positive reaction to mistakes

Looks like an athlete on a mission

Open with a desire to talk with team-mates

The Red Zone in perfectionists

In the Red Zone, immediately you can see the pervasive doubts about the perfectionist's actions and ability that are typically expressed with the thoughts 'Have I done enough?' or 'Am I good enough?' These guiding thoughts maintain the anxiety and contribute to the panic and meltdowns in preparation for big moments. Inside their performance, the perfectionist aims to get everything just right and thinks there is a 'right' way and 'wrong' way to do everything. This leads to indecisiveness, controlled movements and slow reaction time. For the perfectionist, mistakes can be an indication that they are doomed to fail, and motivation can drop very quickly. The perfectionist can be self-critical and destructive inside their performance if it's not going well. This is how a perfectionist can become disinterested, unmotivated and can want to hide away from everyone and everything.

The Green Zone in perfectionists

I can honestly say that 99% of the time when I do the Green Zone analysis with a perfectionist, the first point they highlight is, I can do this! The second point is typically how focused they are on simply what they want to do, one task-at-a-time, or one-point-at-a-time. Perfectionist students often refer to their checklists and how they are mentally or physically checking off the items on their list, one by one in their Green Zone. The positive self-talk and the task focus is so prominent in this zone.

Remarkably, pride is one of the most common feelings I see in the Green Zone for perfectionists. This means it is possible, even natural, for a perfectionist to engage in positive self-talk, and feel confident and empowered. A perfectionist will point out how focused they feel in their Green Zone. Their ability to create fearsome focus and drive is one of their greatest strengths. You might believe that these thoughts are occurring *because* the athlete is performing well that day. But that is not necessarily the case. You see, the perfectionist is still making errors in the Green Zone, and they certainly can't perform *perfectly*, so it's not the results that are causing this positivity. The perfectionist recognises their strength in their work-ethic in the Green Zone. What's more, they are *perfectly* focused on the task at hand, and that allows them to feel in control and unstoppable. One of the most important ingredients in this Green Zone chart is the positive reaction to mistakes the perfectionist demonstrates. This means that even perfectionists can be adaptable and allow room for error. In the 'Actions' column, you can see an athlete who is full of effort and persistence, and the perfectionist can be a brilliant competitor when they achieve this state.

The perfectionist parent

The research indicates that perfectionism is genetic. This means if you are a perfectionist, there is a strong chance that you will transfer your perfectionist tendencies to your child. In the next case, I'll show you the most common fault of perfectionist sport parents.

Case 10: The biggest mistake perfectionist parents make

John came to visit me for a one-to-one session when he realised that his actions toward his daughter Sophia and her performance on the golf course might need adjusting, but he wasn't sure how to go about it. John was concerned that their current interaction was going to affect their relationship and his daughter's relationship with the sport she loves.

He explained, 'I thought our time together was a good opportunity to talk through what she was doing wrong, so she could learn from it. The more resistance Sophia shows, the more frustrated I feel, because I am concerned that she simply isn't learning from her mistakes.'

John's dilemma is that he wants to help his daughter improve and enjoy their time together, but instead, they often end up in a war of emotion.

I notice that perfectionist parents like John have a strong aversion to their athlete's mistakes. For instance, if you are a golf parent watching your child hit balls on the range in practice, you are likely to cringe and react to every miss hit, without being aware that you shrug off the more solid shots because that's simply what you *expect* to see.

Like so many parents who fit this case example, John prioritises the dissection of errors as a way to help his daughter improve. The emphasis placed on fixing and avoiding mistakes is intensified by the fact that John is a perfectionist. He strongly believes that mistakes need to be eradicated and, most notably, he believes you shouldn't make the same mistake twice.

If you are a perfectionist parent or coach, with a strong concern about mistakes, the number one problem you will see when your athlete is competing is poor emotional control. This happens because you have trained them to react badly to mistakes. Before you can support your athlete to be emotionally resilient in competition, you must first adjust your own beliefs and attitudes about mistakes.

If your child is a perfectionist, they are also hard-wired to be concerned over mistakes and doubt their ability. If you focus on the dissection of errors and instil the belief that they shouldn't make the same mistake twice, you will intensify the challenges they face as a perfectionist.

Adjust your attitude and response toward mistakes

During the game is *not* the time for analysing and dissecting errors, no matter if it's a family fun game or a competition. Game time is the time to focus on bouncing back from errors and should be about emphasising positive responses to mistakes, not trying to avoid errors.

Try this: if you have the chance to play a family game, you could challenge each other to see who can respond the most effectively to their mistakes and make a competition out of it. This way, you are training resilience instead of the need for perfection.

After the game, don't waste energy trying to make sure your athlete doesn't make the same mistake twice. When you do this, you are only focusing on the 'situation' and looking at what they could or should do differently next time tactically or technically (reactive solutions). The chances of your athlete being in exactly the same situation again are practically nil.

Try this instead of focusing on tactical and technical solutions. You can ask curious questions to help your athlete understand what they were focused on, thinking about, and what they were doing at the time they made errors. For perfectionists, it comes down to indecisiveness and lack of commitment in the skill, move or shot. Help them realise there is no perfect move, but whatever they choose they need to commit to it. Commitment leads to solid execution of skills and minimises errors. This is how your athlete can start to create proactive habits that support peak performance.

GO TO Chapter 7 – Alternative approach 3: preventing mistakes vs reactive solutions

Debrief the positive actions instead of dissecting mistakes

Instead of dissecting errors when you debrief, always talk about the key habits and gather your athlete's perspective on how strongly they felt they executed these things.

Remember key positive habits include: a fighting spirit, bouncing back from mistakes, focusing on the task, positive self-talk, and consistent routines during breaks in play.

When you debrief about the key habits instead of mistakes, you focus on the factors over which your athlete has a high degree of control. More importantly, these are the actions your athlete can 'do more of' instead of avoiding or trying to 'do less of' in their next event.

GO TO Chapter 6 – How to use a Positive Actions Chart

Supporting the young perfectionist athlete

All the strategies I have introduced in this book can support any young athlete. However, when it comes to perfectionist athletes, these support strategies are not just important, they are crucial.

Top 3 must-dos for parents with perfectionist athletes

- value the process
- capture the Green Zone
- build a mastery-climate.

The must-dos

Value and emphasise the performance process

A perfectionist can thrive when they concentrate their conscientiousness, drive and high standards into developing the key habits in their Performance Process. The perfectionist's efforts and striving are always well placed in this area because these are the ingredients that they can control. Also, peace of mind comes from knowing that high effort in the process leads to big gains.

Don't expect results, strive for results

To keep expectations from becoming unrelated, you should focus on developing high expectations in their process and leave them out of the results. That's not to say the young athlete can't have lofty goals, of course they can! But the results are not expectations or givens. Results are the markers and milestones to strive for, to aim for, to chase after.

GO TO Chapter 1 – The Performance Process

Capture the Green Zone

The best counter-measures for the dark side of perfectionism are found in your athlete's Green Zone. These are the thoughts and actions they engage already when performing at their best. A perfectionist who is confident in their Performance Process will be able to shift from anxious to tenacious in anything they set out to do. If you only use one strategy from this book, make it this one. When an athlete understands they can better control their performance by replicating key thoughts and actions from their Green Zone, they won't look for control with elaborate superstitious habits that have no connection to their performance.

Here is an example in a young golf player. Superstitious habits might involve, 'adjusting the glove twice and tapping the ground three times before every shot'. These actions are distracting, energy draining, and have no bearing on the shot. Instead, the golfer could utilise their Green Zone ingredients, such as focusing their eyes on the target at set up, and deliberately engaging positive self-talk as they walk down the fairway. These actions will lead to the control they are seeking in a way that builds confidence and reduces anxiety.

There are so many positives that can come from building conversations with your athlete about their Green Zone experiences.

GO TO Chapter 2 – Capturing the Green Zone

Build a mastery-climate

In a lot of ways, the striving perfectionist at their best is very similar to a thriving athlete with a mastery-focus. To help support this focus, you must value and praise putting in effort, taking risks and trying new things. Steer clear of comparisons to others and focus on learning and bouncing back from mistakes, rather than expecting error-free performances.

GO TO Chapter 3 – Table 7: A summary of the expectations that are emphasised, the atmosphere and the typical actions by coaches, parents and peers within a mastery-climate

'Go-to strategies' with young perfectionists

To conclude, I want to provide you with 'go-to strategies' to support the biggest challenges young perfectionists face before, during and after the game. Consider this section as a quick reference guide or cheat-sheet, applying various support strategies from this book.

Before the game

Challenge 1: Setting extremely high expectations for the results, focused on achieving perfect performance and/or error free performance.

What you hear and what you see
Your athlete will be anxious and tense in the days leading up to the competition. They could seem moody, short-tempered and tired. You hear, 'I have to perform well', and 'I'm worried I'll perform badly.'

Emphasise the Performance Process *not* just the results

Create focus goals around their key habits that lead to peak performance.

For young perfectionists, the three most important key habits in the process are:

- effort and giving 100% of what you've got on that given day
- responding well to mistakes
- positive self-talk.

If nothing else, you can talk about these key habits, make them the focus goals for their competition, and set rewards for executing them.

Challenge 2: More superstitious habits are emerging, particularly in the days leading up to the competition. Preparation is becoming rigid and tense.

What you hear and what you see

Your athlete might say something like, 'I need to have that special pasta for breakfast, please', or 'I need to take that blue water bottle today and where are those socks, I told you I needed them.' You may feel like you are running a spartan race yourself the morning of a competition! Even if your child is more independent and takes care of these things themselves, you will see panic if certain things aren't in the 'right' place.

How you can help

Superstitious habits stem from a need for control over one's performance. If your athlete ate pasta that one time before a great race, then they may think they *need* it before every race after that. If it takes too much energy and focus to perform the superstitious action every time, or your athlete panics when it's missing, then it's no longer a reassuring little quirk, it's controlling and consuming. The key to reducing superstitious habits is to support a few key ingredients in preparation but keep these broadly in focus and add some variety into the mix. For example, three key ingredients before game time are:

- relaxation activities the night before
- sleep
- healthy breakfast.

Mix up the types of things you do together to help your child relax the night before the game. This will ensure you and your athlete don't get too rigid or seek perfection with these activities. Explain that the key ingredient in preparation is simply relaxation, but there are lots of ways to create it. The same goes for sleep. Move away from exact timing for perfectionists and just reinforce the message that 'whenever you feel sleepy you can go to bed.' It might vary from time to time but that is okay! If your athlete has already trained with consistent sleep and wake timings, then this will be easy. A healthy breakfast is a key ingredient for preparation, but super-specific foods are not necessary, especially for perfectionists. Instead of always preparing the exact same meal, mix up the options that establish the overall healthy breakfast. Adding variety is important for reducing inflexibility. Remember competing well is about adapting, not perfecting. Your athlete still has their key ingredients for great preparation, but variety within these ingredients will reduce demanding superstitions. Over time your perfectionist will feel confident and composed, instead of being rigid and anxious before competing.

Challenge 3: Focusing on all the little things that aren't optimal before big moments.

What you hear and what you see

Panic and meltdowns are common. Before exams, you see last-minute fixing, cramming and revising. Before competitions, you see last minute tweaks to technique and equipment changes. You hear 'I don't feel like I have prepared enough', 'I can't get anything right', or 'I'm going to be terrible'.

How you can help

Building a confidence jar – don't settle on surface-level reassurance such as 'Don't worry, you'll be fine.' Support your athlete to focus on the facts that give them real reasons to trust themselves. Create a list together of the reasons to trust their skills – the things they have improved lately, and the skills they are performing well in training. This is a great go-to strategy.

If you have some time before their next competition, you can introduce the confidence jar. After every training session, your child comes home and puts a note into the jar that describes one thing they did well today, improved or felt proud of, and they build a collection. The night before the competition, they can open that jar and read all the positive points they have collected. It is an incredibly uplifting exercise, and activates trust and confidence based on the facts.

Last-minute preparation rituals

These are things like last-minute fixing techniques in sport or cramming and focusing on the small gaps in knowledge in study. They are some of the unfortunate habits of perfectionists that can derail all confidence and control. If they feel the need to do *some* preparation the night before, help your perfectionist to focus only on practising or revising their strengths, the things they are presently doing well or enjoy. Confidence going in will activate their Green Zone thoughts and effort on the day.

During the Game

Challenge 1: Not letting go of errors and sliding into the Red Zone.

What you hear and what you see
Your athlete is visibly upset and reacting badly to their mistakes. They look to you for instructions and advice on how to fix it. You hear, 'what am I doing wrong?'

Create a signal of encouragement with your athlete
When you are present at competitions, your athlete will look to you more often for reassurance. Before the competition, come up with an agreed gesture or signal of encouragement to give your athlete. The gesture can be as simple as a nod and smile, but your athlete knows that it means, first and foremost, to focus on bouncing back from mistakes and move on to the next point or play. This proactive step is helpful for all young athletes, but especially for young perfectionists.

GO TO Chapter 6 – Signal encouragement

After the Game

Challenge 1: Extreme disappointment, self-criticism, and going over and over mistakes in their mind.

What you hear and what you see
Your athlete experiences emotional breakdowns, hides in their room and does not want to talk to anyone.

How you can help

Your perfectionist will be going over and over in their mind the mistakes they made and the 'could haves' and 'should haves'. Do not prioritise the dissection of errors in your debrief. In fact, don't do it at all, it will not lead to good outcomes. Reviewing only the mistakes creates more frustration and despair.

Parents and coaches often ask me about the right thing to say in those moments, the magic words that can turn things around for their athlete. There are no magic words or statements. To help your child with a productive reflection when they feel disappointed, you must build their awareness of their Performance Process first – the Red Zone and Green Zone – in previous competitions. This allows your athlete to talk through their performances productively, especially the disappointing ones. There are no short-cuts, unfortunately. However, it really only takes three or four post-competition reflections using the questions presented at the end of Chapter 2 to build the awareness for productive reflections after the game.

You don't have to be as structured as the questions imply in Chapter 2. You could start with a casual prompt such as 'It might be good to talk through your Red Zone moments today and see what you can draw out of them for next time.'

Perfectionists can benefit greatly from this type of debrief, because it stops the mistakes circling around on repeat in their minds. It's imperative to listen with curiosity and ask questions, don't give advice in these moments. Allow your athlete to share what they noticed and learnt about themselves. When you connect them with the things they can work on or change in their process for the next match, you help to activate the *striving* part of their perfectionist personality, and they can feel highly motivated following this type of collaborative reflection.

By creating conversations that build your athlete's awareness of these zones, you are supporting the development of the productive assessment of performance in the face of disappointment, which is crucial for perfectionists.

Challenge 2: Never being satisfied with their performance, even a great performance.

What you hear and what you see

Your athlete will say things like, 'It could have been better,' and 'What's next?' Following an exceptional performance, they may seem particularly subdued.

How you can help

If this sort of reaction becomes a habit in their youth, your child can lose their drive and striving as they get older. 'What's next?' becomes 'What's the point?' It is crucial that you guide them to create rituals to pause, reflect and celebrate the small victories together.

Praise the times they take a risk or try new things. Celebrate the effort and tenacity *not* just the results. If your athlete is between six and 12 years of age, celebrating or acknowledging the times they performed their key habits in their process exceptionally well has a strongly positive impact. This is one of the best ways for your athlete to learn to value the process, just as much as they do the results. Simply take a deliberate pause or a quiet moment together to acknowledge the small victories or give praise. A simple reward such as their favourite meal becomes a powerful ritual that carries forward in their career and life. Celebrating the small victories, especially the execution of their high-performance habits, will *not* lead to complacency. Complacency happens when you only focus on the results. Rituals that celebrate high performance habits will build self-compassion and true confidence.

QUICK POINTS

- If you are a perfectionist parent or coach, with a strong concern about mistakes, the number one problem you will see in your athlete when competing will be poor emotional control. Before you can support your athlete to be emotionally resilient in competition, you must first adjust your own beliefs and attitudes about mistakes.
- The best counter measures for the dark side of perfectionism are found in your athlete's Green Zone. When an athlete understands they can better control their performance by replicating key thoughts and actions from their Green Zone, they won't look for control with elaborate superstitious habits or rigid preparation.
- It is crucial that you guide your athlete to create rituals to pause, reflect and celebrate the small victories together. Praise the times they take a risk or try new things. Celebrating the small victories, especially the execution of their high-performance habits, will not lead to complacency. Complacency happens when you only focus on the results.

FINAL POINTS

The case examples I have presented throughout this book capture the distinct experience and challenges your athlete has gone through, is going through, or will go through at some stage in their sport journey, regardless of their level of competition. I strongly believe the cases I have curated here transcend culture and international borders. They are representative of all children, parents and coaches involved in youth sport around the world today and what we will see more of in the next decades. The support strategies and tools I have shared here are also universal. I designed these strategies with all young athletes in mind. Supporting those who are anxious to become adaptable is at the heart of these techniques, but they can also work wonderfully for children who are thriving, and all young athletes in between.

Sport has paved the way for everything in my life. I would not have had the opportunities I have had, the experiences, or the bond I have with my parents, without sport in my life. Playing golf as a junior gave me the opportunity to realise my strengths firsthand and see what I could achieve when I put my mind to it. I can say that I was very much an anxious young athlete, more passionate than confident for sure, and sport was the platform that gave me the opportunity to grow my courage and tenacity. My goal with this book is to make certain that you as a parent, coach or teacher can walk that journey alongside your athlete, and facilitate the extraordinary learnings and growth that are possible.

I acknowledge that the techniques and strategies in this book require a high degree of mindfulness. You need to be intentional and ready to try new things in critical moments. It is much easier to simply give your athlete instructions, corrections and advice from the sidelines and in the car ride home. But you won't build a strong bond with your child through sport this way, or help them to become an adaptable, independent athlete. Collaborative reflections and building a mastery-climate take practice, patience and a willingness to listen to your athlete's thoughts and perspectives.

I talk a lot about learning to understand your athlete's Performance Process, and you can view the strategies in this book as your own process to follow in your supporting role. Once you've read this final page, turn back the pages to Chapter 2 or 3 and pick just one of the questions to ask your athlete during your next car ride home after a game, or even after training. To enhance your mindfulness, before the game, ask yourself, 'How can I show that I value a mastery-focus today?' and 'Which positive habit could I encourage or praise more?'

Always remember that sport should not be transactional, it is, above all else, *emotional*. And with this in mind, always approach your athlete and their performances with empathy. No matter how much you invest (if you are the parent or the athlete), unfortunately, the results are *never* a given.

Understanding this in your supporting role is what it means to respect the sport and your athlete's journey in it. Be ready to celebrate the small victories, alleviate the sting of tough losses, and capture the learnings from difficult mistakes together. Sport is a gift for all young children. And this book is my gift to you.

REFERENCES

Chapter 1

Burgess N. S., Knight C. J. & Mellalieu S. D. (2016). 'Parental stress and coping in elite youth gymnastics: An interpretive phenomenological analysis'. *Qualitative Research in Sport, Exercise and Health*, 8, pp 237–256.

Curran, T. & Hill, A. (2017). 'Perfectionism is Increasing Over Time: A Meta-Analysis of Birth Cohort Differences From 1989 to 2016'. *Psychological Bulletin*. 145, p. 10.

Dorsch T. E., Smith A. L., Wilson S. R. & McDonough M. H. (2015). 'Parent goals and verbal sideline behavior in organized youth sport'. *Sport, Exercise, and Performance Psychology*, 4, pp 19–35.

Elliott, S. K. & Drummond, M. J. N. (2017). 'Parents in youth sport: What happens after the game?'. *Sport, Education and Society*. 22: 3, pp 391–406.

Knight, C. J., Neely, K. C. & Holt, N. L. (2011). 'Parental behaviours in team sports how do female athletes want parents to behave?'. *Journal of Applied Sport Psychology*. 23: 1, pp 76–92.

McMahon J. A. & Penney D. (2015). 'Sporting parents on the pool deck: Living out a sporting culture?'. *Qualitative Research in Sport, Exercise and Health*, 7, pp 153–169.

Chapter 2

Csikszentmihalyi, Mihaly. (1990). 'Flow: The Psychology of Optimal Experience'. *Journal of Leisure Research*, 24: 1, pp 93–94.

Chapter 3

Appleton, P. R., Hall, H. K. & Hill, A. P. (2011). 'Examining the influence of the parent-initiated and coach-created motivational climates upon athletes' perfectionist cognitions'. *Journal of Sports Sciences*, 29, pp 661–671.

Atkins, M. R., Johnson, D. M., Force, E. C. & Petrie, T. A. (2015). 'Peers, parents, and coaches, oh my! The relationship of the motivational climate to boys' intention to continue in sport'. *Psychology of Sport and Exercise,* 16, pp 170–180.

Harwood, C. & Thrower, S. (2020). 'Motivational climate in youth sport groups'. *The Power of Groups in Youth Sport*, pp 145–163.

McLaren D. C., Eys, M. A. & Murray, R. A. (2015). 'A Coach-Initiated Motivational Climate Intervention and Athletes'. *Sport, Exercise, & Performance Psychology*, 4: 2, pp 113–126.

Ommundsen, Y., Roberts, G. C., Lemyre, P. N. & Miller, B. W. (2005). 'Peer relationships in adolescent competitive soccer: Associations to perceived motivational climate, achievement goals and perfectionism'. *Journal of Sports Sciences*, 23, pp 977–989.

O'Rourke, D. J., Smith, R.E., Smoll, F. L., & Sean, P. (2011). 'Trait Anxiety in Young Athletes as a function of Parental Pressure and Motivational Climate: Is Parental Pressure Always Harmful?'. *Journal of Applied Sport Psychology*, 23: 4, pp 398-412.

Smith, R. E., Smoll, F. L., & Cummings, S. P. (2007). 'Effects of motivational climate intervention for coaches on young athletes' sport performance anxiety'. *Journal of Sport & Exercise Psychology*, 28, pp 479–501.

Vazou, S., Ntoumanis, N. & Duda, J. L (2005). 'Peer motivational climate in youth sport: A qualitative inquiry'. *Psychology of Sport and Exercise*, 6, pp 497–516.

Chapter 4

Omli. J. & Wiese-Bjornstal, D. M. (2011). 'Kids Speak'. *Research Quarterly for Exercise and Sport*, 82: 4, pp 702–711.

Tamminen, K. A., Poucher, Z., & Povilaitis, V. (2017). 'The car ride home: An interpretive analysis of parent–child sport conversations'. *Sport, Exercise, and Performance Psychology*, 6: 4, 325339. doi: 10.1037/spy0000093

Chapter 6

Bois J. E., Lalanne, J. & Delforge, C. (2009). 'The influence of parenting practices and parental presence on children's and adolescents' pre-competitive anxiety'. *Journal of Sports Sciences*, 27: 10, pp 995–1005.

Knight C. J. & Holt. N. L. (2014). 'Parenting in youth tennis: Understanding and enhancing children's experiences'. *Psychology of Sport and Exercise*, 15, pp 155–164.

Omli. J. & Wiese-Bjornstal, D. M. (2011). 'Kids Speak'. *Research Quarterly for Exercise and Sport*, 82: 4, pp 702–711.

'Day in the Life: Michael Phelps'. 7 June 2016: owaves.com/day-plan/day-life-michael-phelps/

Chapter 7

Bois J. E., Lalanne, J. & Delforge, C. (2009). 'The influence of parenting practices and parental presence on children's and adolescents' pre-competitive anxiety'. *Journal of Sports Sciences*, 27: 10, pp 995–1005.

Elliott, S. K. & Drummond, M. J. N. (2017). 'Parents in youth sport: what happens after the game?' *Sport, Education and Society*, 22: 3, pp 391–406.

Knight C. J. & Holt. N. L. (2014). 'Parenting in youth tennis: Understanding and enhancing children's experiences'. *Psychology of Sport and Exercise*, 15, pp 155–164

Omli. J. & Wiese-Bjornstal, D. M. (2011). 'Kids Speak'. *Research Quarterly for Exercise and Sport*, 82: 4, pp 702–711.

Tamminen, K. A., Poucher, Z., & Povilaitis, V. (2017). 'The car ride home: An interpretive analysis of parent-child sport conversations'. *Sport, Exercise, and Performance Psychology*, 6: 4, 325339. doi: 10.1037/spy0000093

Chapter 8

Curran, T. & Hill, A. (2019). 'Perfectionism is increasing over time: A meta-analysis of birth cohort differences from 1989 to 2016'. *Psychological Bulletin*, 145: 4, pp 410–429.

Longbottom, J-L., Grove, J. R. & Dimmock, J. A. (2012). 'Trait perfectionism, self-determination, and self-presentation processes in relation to exercise behavior'. *Psychology of Sport and Exercise*, 13, pp 234–235.

Longbottom, J-L., Grove, J. R. & Dimmock, J. A. (2010). 'An examination of perfectionism traits and physical activity motivation'. *Psychology of Sport and Exercise*, 11, pp 574–581.

INDEX

www.ingramcontent.com/pod-product-compliance
Lightning Source LLC
Chambersburg PA
CBHW021140090426
42740CB00008B/871